TWENTIETH CENTURY INTERPRETATIONS
OF
MURDER
IN THE
CATHEDRAL

A Collection of Critical Essays

Edited by
DAVID R. CLARK

Prentice-Hall, Inc. *Englewood Cliffs, N. J.*

A SPECTRUM BOOK

Current printing (last number):
10 9 8 7 6 5 4 3 2 1

PRENTICE-HALL INTERNATIONAL, INC. (*London*)
PRENTICE-HALL OF AUSTRALIA, PTY. LTD. (*Sydney*)
PRENTICE-HALL OF CANADA, LTD. (*Toronto*)
PRENTICE-HALL OF INDIA PRIVATE LIMITED (*New Delhi*)
PRENTICE-HALL OF JAPAN, INC. (*Tokyo*)

To the Martyrs, 1170–1970

"We are not to think of a martyr as primarily one who suffers for a cause, or who gives up his life for truth, but as a witness to the awful reality of the supernatural."

—HELEN GARDNER, *The Art of T. S. Eliot* (New York: E. P. Dutton & Co., Inc., 1949). Reprinted by permission of E. P. Dutton & Co., Inc., and the Cresset Press, London.

Contents

Introduction

by David R. Clark

T. S. Eliot was born at 2635 Locust Street in St. Louis, Missouri, on September 26, 1888. He was the youngest of the seven children of Henry Ware Eliot (1843–1919), a successful manufacturer who became president of the Hydraulic Brick Company, and Charlotte Champe Stearns (1843–1929), daughter of a Boston tradesman.

Of Puritan New England ancestry, Eliot eventually became a British subject and declared himself a "classicist in literature, royalist in politics and anglo-catholic in religion." [1] There is some connection, as one critic seems to imply, between the locale of the poet's birth and the fact that he "would one day adopt most of the traditions represented by the town of St. Louis, founded by the French under Louis XIV—royalist, Latin, Catholic traditions which recall Ignatius Loyola rather than Calvin, Thomas Aquinas rather than Emerson." [2] The place where he was born and grew up, however, had less effect on his development than his remarkable family. It is hard to escape the view that when drawing the character of Archbishop Thomas à Becket, who, in *Murder in the Cathedral*, so radically maintained his conservative view of the rights of the Church against a powerful King, Eliot created a likeness to several family members.

A recent study of Eliot's background, Herbert Howarth's *Notes on Some Figures Behind T. S. Eliot*,[3] convinced the reader that much of Eliot's work has been a reassertion of family-held values. The "East Coker" section of *Four Quartets* perhaps rationalizes Eliot's search through ancestors such as Andrew Eliot (1627–1704), who migrated to Massachusetts from East Coker, Somerset, in 1670, and fountainheads of English tradition (thoroughly classical, royalist and Anglo-Catholic)

---

[1] In the "Preface" to *For Lancelot Andrewes* (London: Faber & Gwyer, 1928), p. ix.
[2] George Cattaui, *T. S. Eliot,* trans. Claire Pace & Jean Stewart (New York: Funk & Wagnalls, 1968), p. 3.
[3] Herbert Howarth, *Notes on Some Figures behind T. S. Eliot* (Boston: Houghton Mifflin Company, 1964). I am much indebted to Howarth's book in this introduction.

1

such as Sir Thomas Elyot, author of *A Boke Named the Governour*, in
1531. Eliot's immediate forbears, some of them Unitarian preachers
and social reformers, no doubt had a more direct, though less visible,
effect on his work. For example, the household of his uncle, Thomas
Lamb Eliot, who started the Unitarian Church of Our Father in Portland, Oregon, provided a model of a daily and yearly round of religious
observance long before Eliot had heard of Nicholas Ferrar, whose
seventeenth-century retreat, where Charles I found shelter, he memo-
rialized in "Little Gidding." In this uncle, in his mother, and in his
paternal grandfather, Eliot found a commitment to the value of Christian witness that was essentially expressed in Thomas à Becket's sermon
in *Murder in the Cathedral*.

In 1834, the poet's grandfather, William Greenleaf Eliot (1811–1887),
a graduate of Harvard Divinity School, moved to St. Louis to found the
first Unitarian church there. He was conservative, he valued the Christian tradition as expressed in other churches, and he respected the in-
stitutions of baptism and the Lord's Supper.[4] He took his stand for the
martyrs, not only of the past, but also of the contemporary crisis. "The
blood of the martyr is the seed not only of the Church, but of truth
and liberty," he declared [5] in commemoration of a martyred protester,
Elijah Lovejoy, who was driven out of Saint Louis and later murdered
because of his forthright stand against slavery. Tempted to the martyr's
role himself, William Eliot once challenged the mistreatment of a
woman slave, once successfully freed a runaway slave, Archer Alex-
ander, in spite of the fugitive slave law, and on many occasions spoke
out against slavery. At first he avoided speaking from the pulpit, which
would have resulted in futile dismissal and a return East. He felt that
he must sacrifice comfortable martyrdom in order to gain influence.
When he finally spoke from the pulpit at the outbreak of the Civil War,
he took the position of gradual emancipation and unconditional support of the Union. No martyrdom ensued, but one-fourth of his con-
gregation left his church. Clearly, he actively helped to keep Missouri
in the Union.

Earlier, he had shown the combination of priest and administrator
that is exhibited in Eliot's Thomas. "The whole city was his parish and
every soul needing him a parishioner" reads his monument,[6] and he
had lived up to that tribute by energetic and sacrificial help to the unfortunate, efforts that were redoubled during the cholera attack of 1849.
Interesting himself in education, he helped to make the Saint Louis

---

[4] Howarth, p. 12.
[5] Howarth, p. 6.
[6] Howarth, p. 2.

schools remarkable in the nation, and his energy created Washington University, of which he became chancellor in 1872. During the war, he made an extraordinary success of organizing non-partisan relief and hospital services through the Western Sanitary Commission. He fought for prohibition, for women's rights, and against prostitution, making real gains at whatever he attempted. T. S. Eliot, in an address at Washington University, said that in his childhood home, "The standard of conduct was that which my grandfather had set; our moral judgments, our decisions between duty and self-indulgence, were taken as if, like Moses, he had brought down the tables of the Law, any deviation from which would be sinful." [7] Eliot's mother was devoted to the memory of her father-in-law, and she wrote his biography.[8] When one reads the seventy-six-year-old grandfather's poem, "Nunc Dimittis," which is somewhat anticipatory of Eliot's "Song for Simeon," one is further convinced that this remarkable forbear was often in his grandson's mind when ideal behavior was the subject of his thought.[9]

Eliot's uncle, Thomas Lamb Eliot, reproduced his father's image in his Portland ministry, serving the unfortunate and fighting for social reform. Howarth produces passages to show that he too "thought constantly of the martyrs." [10] Although Eliot's father, the second son, restored the balance by choosing a different image and by becoming a wealthy manufacturer of bricks and sewer-pipes, Eliot's mother was, in her prime, an ardent social reformer, prison reformer, and champion of women's rights. (Eliot's eldest sister, Ada, under this influence, became a leading professional social worker.) A religious commitment was the basis of Mrs. Eliot's activities and of her poems about the saints and martyrs, including one about the martyred philosopher Giordano Bruno.[11] Her poem *Savonorola* was published in 1926 in London with an introduction by T. S. Eliot. Savonorola is another figure who died a martyr to the principle that the law of God supersedes the law of man, who rejected worldly honors and power, and who, like Thomas, forced his followers to disarm themselves and "unbar the door" to enemies.[12]

---

[7] T. S. Eliot, *American Literature and the American Language* (St. Louis: Washington University Press, 1953), Appendix, p. 29. Later reprinted in T. S. Eliot, *To Criticize the Critic* (New York: Farrar Straus & Giroux, Inc., 1965).
[8] C. C. Eliot, *William Greenleaf Eliot* (Boston: 1904).
[9] Howarth, pp. 10–11.
[10] Howarth, p. 14.
[11] Howarth, p. 31. Compare the use of Mary Queen of Scots' sentiment "In my end is my beginning" in Eliot's "East Coker" with these lines by his mother: "Mysterious power that mouldest to thy will! / In the beginning seest thou the end, / And in the end a mere beginning still."
[12] Cf. Howarth, p. 32.

II

Eliot attended the Smith Academy in St. Louis, from 1898 to 1905, was graduated from the Milton Academy in Milton, Massachusetts, in 1906, and from Harvard University in 1910. At Harvard, medieval history taught by Charles Homer Haskins and ancient and medieval Latin poetry taught by E. K. Rand (both teachers he later praised) gave him a foundation for his readings in the Middle Ages, for his studies of Dante, and for writing *Murder in the Cathedral.* In the next years, he studied philosophy at the Sorbonne, Harvard, very briefly at Marburg, Germany, and at Merton College, Oxford.

Eliot was married on June 26, 1915, to Vivienne Haigh Haigh-Wood, a ballet dancer and daughter of the painter Charles Haigh Haigh-Wood. The marriage had an unhappy history. Sir Herbert Read recalls that Mrs. Eliot was "sweet and vivacious" but a "frail creature" of a "nervous temperament" who "slowly but surely developed the hysterical psychosis to which she finally succumbed." Eliot's growing marital troubles resulted in a formal separation in 1933. One undoubtedly finds in the asceticism of Ash-Wednesday (1930)—the first edition of which is dedicated to Mrs. Eliot—and in Thomas's dismissal of the first tempter in *Murder in the Cathedral* a reflection of Eliot's mood during this difficult period. Herbert Read implies that Eliot remained single on principle as long as Mrs. Eliot lived.[13] She died in a nursing home in 1947 after a long illness. In 1957, Eliot married his private secretary, Esmé Valerie Fletcher and, in Stephen Spender's words, "achieved with his radiant wife the happiness which had been denied him during most of his maturity, a happiness of which one guesses he had glimpses as a child." [14]

After his first marriage in 1915, Eliot became a teacher of French, mathematics, history, geometry, art, and swimming at High Wycombe Grammar School, and later at the Highgate School, where he stayed for four terms. Exhausted by the teaching profession, Eliot accepted a position in Lloyd's bank that he kept until 1925, when he entered the publishing firm of Faber and Gwyer, later Faber and Faber.

Eliot's first volume of poems, *Prufrock and Other Observations,* appeared in 1917, and his first book of criticism, *The Sacred Wood,* in 1920. The latter showed his great interest in verse drama of the Eliza-

[13] Sir Herbert Read, "T. S. E.—A Memoir," *T. S. Eliot, The Man and His Work,* ed. Allen Tate (New York: Dell Publishing Co., n. d.), p. 23.
[14] Stephen Spender, "Remembering Eliot," *T. S. Eliot, the Man and His Work,* ed. Tate, p. 60.

bethan past and in the possibilities of verse drama for the future. It was as editor of *The Criterion* and author of the controversial poem *The Waste Land,* which appeared in Volume 1, Number 1 (October 1922), that Eliot began his rule as the most influential poet and critic of the first half of the twentieth century.

The Waste Land was found to express the disillusionment of the post-war generation, a sense of a chaos of values, of a disintegrating civilization. The poem spoke to and for many (such as the Marxist critics) who would later find little sympathy with Eliot's specifically Christian affirmations. For Eliot, the poem was a personal expression of a sense of spiritual sterility, an attempt to shore fragments against his ruins. If disillusionment was the theme, it was disillusionment not so much with the post-war world as with, simply, the world. "The Hollow Men" (1925) is perhaps the nadir of this phase. "Journey of the Magi" (1927) moves upward with its mood of a quest for spiritual fulfillment. "Salutation" (1929, later Part II of *Ash-Wednesday*), his "Dante" essay (1929), "Animula" (1929), and finally the complete *Ash-Wednesday* (1930) are further documents of Eliot's spiritual, as well as artistic, progress.

Ash-Wednesday, with the struggles of a soul to come to terms with its past life and to turn towards God as its theme, is a triumphant artistic achievement and suggests, at least, some sort of gain in the author's spiritual combat. The lines at the end of the poem

> Teach us to sit still
> Even among these rocks,
> Our peace is in His will

relate to the main theme of Dante—*la sua voluntade è nostra pace*—and to the words Eliot was to give to Thomas, "I shall no longer act or suffer, to the sword's end."

After 1930, Eliot often spoke as a convert who had accepted the responsibility of public defense and the promulgation of his beliefs. Such is the tone of "Thoughts after Lambeth" (1931) and *After Strange Gods, A Primer of Modern Heresy* (1934), the latter being a series of lectures given at the University of Virginia in 1933. "Thoughts after Lambeth" ends with this pronouncement: "The World is trying the experiment of attempting to form a civilized but non-Christian mentality. The experiment will fail; but we must be very patient in awaiting its collapse; meanwhile redeeming the time: so that the Faith may be preserved alive through the dark ages before us; to renew and rebuild civilization, and save the World from suicide." [15] Later works

---

[15] T. S. Eliot, *Selected Essays 1917–1932* (New York: Harcourt, Brace and Company, 1932), p. 332.

that turned a Christian eye upon the weaknesses of society and attempted to preserve the Faith were, *The Idea of a Christian Society* (1939), *Notes Toward the Definition of Culture* (1948), some of the essays in *Essays Ancient and Modern* (1936), and *The Rock* (1934).

The Rock is "A Pageant Play Written For Performance At Sadler's Wells Theatre, 28 May–9 June 1934, On Behalf Of The Forty-Five Churches Fund, Of the Diocese of London." [16] Eliot provided the "Book of Words" for a scenario by E. Martin Browne. After its success, the Friends of Canterbury Cathedral asked Eliot to write a play for their annual festival of June 1935. *Murder in the Cathedral* was performed in the Chapter House of the Cathedral, and the first published issue (May 10, 1935) was sold at the performances.

Eliot had long been occupied with the problem of poetic drama in modern times. *Sweeney Agonistes, Fragments of an Aristophanic Melodrama* (1932) had been an experiment in writing on serious themes in a farcical music-hall style, but *Murder in the Cathedral* was Eliot's first independent full-length play. Its success—it later had several good runs in London theaters—interested Eliot in the problem of reaching a wide audience for his poetry and beliefs, so he went on to experiment with plays in contemporary settings and in verse that was superficially like the prose dialogue of more conventional drawing room comedies: *The Family Reunion* (1939), *The Cocktail Party* (1949), *The Confidential Clerk* (1953), and *The Elder Statesman* (1958).

Unused fragments from *Murder in the Cathedral* became the nucleus of "Burnt Norton" which appeared in the *Collected Poems 1909–1935* (1936), and which became the first of the *Four Quartets* (1943). As *The Waste Land* captured Eliot's response to the shock of World War I and its aftermath, so *Four Quartets*, with its evocation in "Little Gidding" of London during an air raid, captured his response to World War II.

> The dove descending breaks the air
> With flame of incandescent terror.

The poem has a much more social and national sense than did *Ash-Wednesday* and not only expresses again the individual's coming to terms with his past, enduring a spiritual crisis, and attempting to turn toward God, but also expresses a people's sense of history, the religious significance of a nation's past and of its present crisis.

> And all shall be well and
> All manner of thing shall be well
> When the tongues of flame are in-folded

[16] T. S. Eliot, *The Rock* (London: Faber & Faber Limited, 1934).

Into the crowned knot of fire
And the fire and the rose are one.

This expression of trust and confidence in the midst of suffering is both
appropriate and remarkable considering that England was enduring
some of the worst moments of the war in October 1942 when "Little
Gidding" appeared.

In his later years, Eliot was honored with some of the world's most
distinguished awards, including the Nobel prize for literature in 1948.
He died in London on January 4, 1965, and is buried in Westminster
Abbey.

III

Eliot's *Murder in the Cathedral* has so far sustained the most continuing interest of his plays, and it will probably prove to be the play
that best withstands the test of time. This success is not merely a matter
of quality, although many critics say that *Murder in the Cathedral* is
Eliot's best play, but also a matter of the perdurability of its theme and
the careful excision of ephemeral appeal in the structure and style.
Eliot has not written an historical play, though he is surprisingly accu-
rate, but instead has presented the unique and idiosyncratic Thomas à
Becket—a very colorful person—as an archetypal figure, the religious
martyr, who wrestles with an archetypal problem, the subtle temptations of the religious conscience when it has set itself up against the
state. Truth of character is gained not by a full portrayal of Thomas in
all his rich personality, but by the precision and sensitivity with which
Eliot delineates the mental struggles of any great and religious man in
his archetypal situation.

The structure of the plot and the advancement of the action follow
a pattern of religious ritual, and the play is most moving—at least to
this spectator—when performed in a church. Like *The Cocktail Party,*
Murder in the Cathedral examines and celebrates an act of sacrifice,
but it does so before the altar, not in a drawing room, and, thus, it lays
claim to the many centuries of both Christian giving and Christian
posturing before that altar. Thomas's death becomes a ritual imitation
or reenactment of the crucifixion of Christ. The fusing of contemporary
poetic idiom with echoes of the language of the medieval morality play
Everyman, sets forth the eternal and universal moral struggle in which
any man who is obliged by circumstance to choose between life and in-
tegrity participates.

Eliot, apparently, did not start *Murder in the Cathedral* from a delib-
erate parallel with a specific Greek tragedy, as he did with his later
plays (the *Oresteia* of Aeschylus in *The Family Reunion*, the *Alcestis* of
Euripides in *The Cocktail Party*, the *Ion* of Euripides in *The Confidential Clerk*, and the *Oedipus at Colonus* of Sophocles in *The Elder
Statesman*). Nevertheless, in no other play in English is the use of the
chorus (here of the "Woman of Canterbury") closer to the use of the
chorus in Greek tragedy. Yet this use is no quaint archaism. We are
reminded of the war-ravaged *Trojan Women* of Euripides, or of the
Nereides, in Aeschylus' *Prometheus Bound*, who ultimately choose to
associate themselves with Prometheus in enduring the vengeance of
Zeus. The chorus fears the results of Thomas's intransigence as the
Theban elders fear Antigone's, and they are as inspirited by Thomas's
sacrifice as, in Sophocles' play, those old men are by hers. The urgency
of Antigone, bound to bury her traitor brother in spite of the king's
edict, is the urgency of Thomas returning to his flock to oppose the
king's will, and her temptation to arrogance is his temptation.

Perhaps these reminiscences of Greek tragedy set into motion a
further allusion to the trial and death of Socrates. Thomas's situation
has parallels with that of Socrates, and perhaps Thomas's arguments
with his tempters are somewhat like parts of the Platonic dialogues,
which owed their form to Greek tragedy. Certainly Thomas's sermon
and some of his final words—

> I give my life
> To the Law of God above the Law of Man

—bring to mind the position taken up by Socrates in the *Apology*:
"Men of Athens, I respect and love you; but I shall obey the god rather
than you. . . ." [17] Thomas's knights, believing that they are only doing
what must be done for the realm's peace, may be compared to Socrates'
judges; and some of Socrates' twitting of his judges could be applied
to the Rotarian speeches of the knights as they justify the assassination.
As will be seen, even the argument that Thomas committed suicide is
anticipated in the *Crito*, when Socrates refuses to take advantage of his
opportunity to escape execution.

Eliot, then, has chosen a subject that is perennial, has made Thomas
an archetypal figure, has structured the play as a ritual sacrifice like
that of the Mass, and has used techniques and language that direct the

[17] *Plato, With an English Translation*, I, *Euthyphro, Apology, Crito, Phaedo,
Phaedrus*, by Harold North Fowler (Cambridge, Massachusetts: Harvard University
Press; London: William Heinemann Ltd., 1943), p. 109.

reader's mind toward, not the *man* Thomas, but toward the figure of suffering conscience trying to be true to itself and to act in the world. For these reasons, the play is as effective today as it was in 1935 and will remain effective in years to come.

IV

The chronology of events in Eliot's life and in contemporary history reveals how close the play was to issues current in 1935. Though probably most of Eliot's audience and readers, then and now, would believe, with the Third Knight, in "a just subordination of the pretensions of the Church to the welfare of the State," most would also firmly approve the struggles, beginning in 1934 (and possibly reflected in Eliot's theme), of the German Confessional Church against Adolf Hitler's interference in ecclesiastical matters—an interference that led to the imprisonment of Pastor Martin Niemöller in 1937. The play is also relevant to an age of assassination like our own. No one who takes leadership in social change today can be sure that he will not go the way of John Fitzgerald Kennedy, Martin Luther King, Robert Kennedy, Malcolm X, Medgar Evers, Andrew Goodman, Ralph Featherstone, and a host of others. One must, therefore, make very sure that he is doing the right deed and for the right reason.

Of the deaths mentioned above, that of Martin Luther King is probably closest to the archetype that Eliot presents in the death of his Thomas, and there is, I think, some virtue in exploring this archetype. Like Thomas, King considered his leadership a spiritual one, knew that he would betray his God, himself, and his followers if he did the right deed for the wrong reason, which is to say, in the wrong spirit—one of pride and aggressiveness rather than one of humility and perseverance in duty. There is a remarkable parallel between King, who countenanced only non-violent resistance to racial injustice and Eliot's Thomas who cries (the poet is following historical sources here):

Unbar the doors! throw open the doors!
I will not have the house of prayer, the church of Christ,
The sanctuary, turned into a fortress. . . .
We are not here to triumph by fighting, by stratagem, or by resistance,
Not to fight with beasts as men. We have fought the beast
And have conquered. We have only to conquer
Now, by suffering.

In his last public talk in Memphis on April 3, 1968, the day before he was assassinated, King's words were much like these. His life had been threatened, but like Thomas he had reached the stillness of peace, and even though he was in Memphis for action—to lead a non-violent demonstration in support of striking sanitation workers—he felt that he would "no longer act or suffer, to the sword's end."

> Well, I don't know what will happen now. We've got some difficult days ahead. But it really doesn't matter with me now. Because I've been to the mountain top. I won't mind.
> Like anybody, I would like to live a long life. Longevity has its place. But I'm not concerned about that now. I just want to do God's will.[18]

As Thomas puts it:

> A martyr, a saint, is always made by the design of God, for His love of men, to warn them and to lead them, to bring them back to His ways. A martyrdom is never the design of man; for the true martyr is he who has become the instrument of God, who has lost his will in the will of God, not lost it but found it, for he has found freedom in submission to God.

Eliot's most uncanny insight into the archetypal situation of martyrdom appears in the Knights' speeches, after they have killed Thomas. The martyr's motivation, Eliot knows, will be misinterpreted, twisted, explained away as "Suicide while of Unsound Mind." Even friends will fail to understand, as Crito insisted to Socrates when the latter refused to escape his punishment,

> It seems to me the thing you are undertaking to do is not even right—betraying yourself when you might save yourself. And you are eager to bring upon yourself just what your enemies would wish and just what those were eager for who wished to destroy you. . . . You seem to me to be choosing the laziest way; and you ought to choose as a good and brave man would choose, you who have been saying all your life that you cared for virtue. So I am ashamed both for you and for us, your friends. . . .[19]

If friends misunderstand, opponents will surely put one's actions in an unfavorable light. A United States senator who confessed that he was "not an admirer of Dr. Martin Luther King" gave in the Senate, the day after King's death, an address that should sufficiently remind us of the archetype, concluding, like the Fourth Knight, that this martyr has brought his own death upon his head.

> . . . I regret, as much as any Senator regrets, the tragedy that befell [Dr. King], and I feel sorrow for his family. I was shocked but I was not sur-

---

[18] *Martin Luther King Memorial* (New York: Country Wide Publications, 1968), p. 44.
[19] *Plato*, p. 159.

prised at what happened, because of the tension that existed in Memphis. . . .

There is a lesson to be drawn from what happened in Memphis and from what has been happening with increasing intensity throughout the Nation in recent years. That is, that mass protests, mass demonstrations, and mass marches and the like—whether labeled nonviolent or otherwise —can only serve to encourage unrest and disorder, and to provoke violence and bloodshed.

And, in the end, those who advocate such methods often become, themselves, the victims of the forces they themselves have set in motion.

This, in a manner, is what happened to Dr. King. He usually spoke of nonviolence. Yet, violence all too often attended his actions. And, at the last, he himself met a violent end. . . .

Dr. King must have known that, rioting having erupted from last week's attempted march in Memphis, there was, in its wake, such an atmosphere of tension as to make his presence in that city dangerous to himself and to others, at least for the time being. He must have known that the situation was volatile, and that passions had become greatly inflamed.

Yet, I regret he persisted in his course, continued to exhort his following to renew the march next week, and told the cheering audiences that a Federal court injunction would be ignored. "We're not going to let any injunction turn us around," he said, according to press reports.

Mr. President, no man can determine for himself whether or not a court injunction is legal or illegal, constitutional or unconstitutional. To do so would be to take the law into one's own hands.

Justice Frankfurter said:

If one man can be allowed to determine for himself what is law, every man can. That means, first, chaos, then tyranny.

Mr. President, one cannot preach nonviolence and, at the same time, advocate defiance of the law, whether it be a court order, a municipal ordinance, or a State or Federal statute. For to defy the law is to invite violence, especially in a tense atmosphere involving many hundreds or thousands of people. To invite violence is to endanger one's own life. And one cannot live dangerously always.

Paul said, in his Epistle to the Romans:

Let every soul be subject unto the higher powers. . . .

Thus, we are exhorted to obey the law and to respect authority, Mr. President, and those who refuse to do this cause serious risks to themselves and to others. . . .

Neither men nor mobs can continue to create disorder and disregard the laws and disrupt the orderly functioning of government at any level, without shaking the very foundations of our society, tearing our country asunder, and destroying themselves in the end.[20]

[20] Senator Robert C. Byrd in the Senate on April 5, 1968. *Congressional Record,* Volume 114, Part 7, pp. 9139–40.

It is difficult to read these words without recalling what the Fourth Knight says of Thomas. A leader who could have brought the country "the unity, the stability, order, tranquillity, and justice that it so badly needed," he instead "showed himself to be utterly indifferent to the fate of the country, to be, in fact, a monster of egotism, a menace to society."

> *Fourth Knight.* . . . He used every means of provocation; from his conduct, step by step, there can be no inference except that he had determined upon a death by martyrdom. This man, formerly a great public servant, had become a wrecker. Even at the last, he could have given us reason: you have seen how he evaded our questions. And when he had deliberately exasperated us beyond human endurance, he could still have easily escaped; he could have kept himself from us long enough to allow our righteous anger to cool. That was just what he did not wish to happen; he insisted, while we were still inflamed with wrath, that the doors should be opened. Need I say more? I think, with these facts before you, you will unhesitatingly render a verdict of Suicide while of Unsound Mind. It is the only charitable verdict you can give, upon one who was, after all, a great man.
>
> *First Knight.* Thank you, Brito. I think that there is no more to be said; and I suggest that you now disperse quietly to your homes. Please be careful not to loiter in groups at street corners, and do nothing that might provoke any public outbreak.

The dilemma of the martyr is not new; Eliot's grandfather was very much aware of it in the years before the Civil War, when he had to determine whether it was right to disobey the Fugitive Slave Law in obedience to the higher law of God.

> For all his feelings against slavery, Dr. Eliot saw infinite dangers in the Higher Law doctrine. Once you conceded its applicability in one instance, where else might not your friends, where else might not your enemies, claim it? Might not someone invoke it to justify secession if his sense of the Higher Law of freedom were hurt? It might become the sanction of fragmentation and anarchy.[21]

This is the truth that the Knights affirm so stoutly in the play. Thomas insisted, had insisted ever since he became Archbishop, "that there was a higher order than that which our King, and he as the King's servant, had for so many years striven to establish; and that—God knows why —the two orders were incompatible." From the Knights' point of view —by putting his own conscience before "the fate of the country"—

---

[21] Howarth, p. 345.

Thomas threatened to bring back the "utter chaos" that, as Chancellor, he had turned into order.

Dr. Eliot's solution of his personal dilemma was remarkably like the reasoning of Socrates. The Higher Law, he declared,

> may, though rarely, "stand in direct conflict with the 'authorities that be,' and peremptorily set them aside at whatever cost." Only, it was a last resort; and if it included *violent* resistance to the State it was a sin against God (even for the martyr to offer violent resistance was a sin against God); and having made his stand, the protester was under the moral obligation to compensate his disobedience to the State by paying the penalty, whether with his wealth, his property, his freedom, his life as the laws of the State required, and only by suffering patiently could he justify what he had done. Thus a man who protected a runaway slave might buy the man's freedom by paying for it or suffering for it.[22]

In Eliot's treatment of Thomas, Herbert Howarth finds a point of view consistent with his grandfather's formulation of the principle of civil disobedience.

> His Becket is a martyr, and every martyr appeals to the Higher Law. Becket appeals rightly, in two senses: he has indeed heard and answered a higher claim than his King's; and he affirms his position in the obligatory way, refraining from violence and offering all he has and all his capacity for suffering to redress the disorder his act involves. And I rather think . . . that Eliot's view of the relationship of Church and State implies the possibility of frequently renewed appeals to the Higher Law. The law of the land strives to represent, as well as human frailty allows, the law of God. But since perfect legislation is not within human power, and since the application of our imperfect laws will tend to yet more devious imperfection, the Church will constantly watch the State and call it back when it deviates; and since the Church is also liable to human error, she too must sometimes be recalled to her strict endeavors. Whenever the recall is uttered, it will sound, to the administrators whose action is either stayed or urged by it, like a presumptuous appeal to the Higher Law. Yet it is necessary. Only it is to be made with prudence as earnest as Dr. Eliot's, and with his acceptance of its terms.[23]

[22] Howarth, p. 346.
[23] Howarth, p. 347.

PART ONE

The Pattern

T. S. Eliot: The Wheel and the Point

by Louis L. Martz

Marianne Moore once acutely remarked that Eliot's poems "are so consistently intricated that one rests on another and is involved with what was earlier." Thus *Four Quartets* rests firmly on a basis of imagery and theme built up by Eliot's other works; and this may be said of all his poems: any given one is best apprehended in the context provided by the body of Eliot's achievement. This is true of all poets in some degree; indeed, assessing the degree of "intrication" among a poet's various works may be one element in deciding the problem of greatness. With these concerns in mind, I should like to explore Eliot's symbol of "the still point," the dominant symbol of his poetry since *The Waste Land,* and at the same time to stress the significance of *Murder in the Cathedral.*

The relation of this play to the core of Eliot's poetry is shown in Becket's first words, addressed to the priest who has been rebuking the Chorus for its lamentations:

> Peace. And let them be, in their exaltation.
> They speak better than they know, and beyond your understanding.
> They know and do not know, what it is to act or suffer.
> They know and do not know, that acting is suffering
> And suffering is action. Neither does the actor suffer

"*T. S. Eliot: The Wheel and the Point.*" Abridged from The Poem of the Mind: Essays on Poetry English and American (*New York: Oxford University Press, 1966*), *pp. 105–24.* Copyright © *1966 by Louis L. Martz.* First published as "*The Wheel and the Point: Aspects of Imagery and Theme in Eliot's Later Poetry*" in The Sewanee Review (*Winter 1947*), *pp. 126–47.* Copyright *1947 by the University of the South. Later expanded in* T. S. Eliot: A Selected Critique, *ed. Leonard Unger (New York, Toronto: Rinehart and Company, Inc., 1948), pp. 444–62. Copyright 1948 by Leonard Unger. Reprinted by permission of Oxford University Press, Inc., the author,* The Sewanee Review, *and Leonard Unger.*

Nor the patient act. But both are fixed
In an eternal action, an eternal patience
To which all must consent that it may be willed
And which all must suffer that they may will it,
That the pattern may subsist, for the pattern is the action
And the suffering, that the wheel may turn and still
Be forever still.

A pattern of double meaning resides in the words, *suffering, patient,* and *patience. Suffering* is not simply *undergoing misery* or *pain;* it is also *permitting, consenting;* he who consents to an action must suffer for it, must accept responsibility for it. The Chorus of Women of Canterbury, the "type of the common man," understands no such responsibility as the play begins: "For us, the poor, there is no action, / But only to wait and to witness." It is this responsibility that the women strive to evade as they realize they are being "drawn into the pattern of fate"; this is what they finally admit at their great moment of exaltation and vision: "I have consented, Lord Archbishop, have consented." It is the admission of sin which Eliot describes and demands in his prose writings—in the essay on Baudelaire's *Journaux Intimes,* for example, where he insists that "the recognition of the reality of Sin is a New Life," and finds the greatness of Baudelaire (like the greatness of the Chorus here) to reside in his capacity for suffering pain in the knowledge of good which comes from the knowledge of evil. It is the view expressed in one of Eliot's notes to *The Idea of a Christian Society*: "The notion of communal responsibility, of the responsibility of every individual for the sins of the society to which he belongs, is one that needs to be more firmly apprehended."

Thus, too, the *patient* is everyone, martyr, murderer, and spectator: he is at once suffering pain and permitting action; in Becket and the Chorus, he is also self-controlled. The same ideas are seen in the lyric of "East Coker," where the "hospital" patient is saved by Christ from "Adam's curse": Beneath the bleeding hands we feel / The sharp compassion of the healer's art." Becket is the Christ of his age, who by suffering heals those who also suffer, as he explains just before his martyrdom:

We are not here to triumph by fighting, by stratagem, or by resistance,
Not to fight with beasts as men. We have fought the beast
And have conquered. We have only to conquer
Now, by suffering. This is the easier victory.
Now is the triumph of the Cross, now
Open the door!

This eternally decreed pattern of suffering, which is also action, and of action, which is also suffering, Eliot symbolizes by the image of the wheel which always turns, yet, at the axis, always remains still. This image lies at the heart of Eliot's poetry. In *Ash Wednesday*:

> Against the Word the unstilled world still whirled
> About the centre of the silent Word.

In the two *Coriolan* poems:

> O hidden under the dove's wing, hidden in the turtle's breast,
> Under the palmtree at noon, under the running water
> At the still point of the turning world. O hidden.

Above all, in the two fragments from Heraclitus which preface "Burnt Norton" and announce the theme of all the *Four Quartets*. The first fragment is closely related to the above passage from *Ash Wednesday*: "But though the Word is common [*central,* in Eliot's image], the many live as though they had a wisdom of their own." The wheel image is more clearly suggested in the second fragment, which is best read with the fragment (LXX) and editorial note immediately following in the Loeb Library edition, for the words of Fragment LXX echo throughout the *Four Quartets*:

LXIX. The road up and the road down is one and the same.
LXX. The beginning and end are common.
   Heraclitus is referring to a point on the circumference of a circle.

These fragments appear in "The Dry Salvages": "And the way up is the way down, the way forward is the way back"; but the image of the wheel is presented most extensively in Section II of "Burnt Norton," opening with the image of "the bedded axle-tree," and continuing with the familiar words:

> At the still point of the turning world. Neither flesh nor fleshless;
> Neither from nor towards; at the still point, there the dance is,
> But neither arrest nor movement.

Here is *Peace*—Becket's first word in the play—the end which all patients and actors in the play, guided or misguided, seek after in their various ways: the Knights by violent worldly action: the Priests by flight and barricade; the Chorus by an attempt to remain unconscious, inactive, seeking a "peace" which is only the refuge of animals: "And the labourer bends to his piece of earth, earth-colour, his own colour,/ Preferring to pass unobserved"; Becket alone by the true path of con-

scious submission to the central Word, as explained by his definition of
Peace in the Christmas sermon. Becket's death is thus the still point of
the world that turns within the play.

This is the theme which unifies Eliot's poetry from the words of
Buddha and St. Augustine in *The Waste Land* to "the unimaginable
zero summer," the still point symbolized by the ascetic ritual of Little
Gidding. Becket and the religious community of Nicholas Ferrar have
for Eliot much the same symbolic meaning—a meaning also found by
Eliot in Pascal and the religious community of Port-Royal. Indeed, the
implication of the whole body of Eliot's writing is nowhere better illustrated than in the interrelation between *Murder in the Cathedral,*
"Little Gidding," and Eliot's essay on the *Pensées* of Pascal. Becket,
Ferrar, and Pascal are, as this essay suggests, symbols of "one kind of
religious believer, which is highly passionate and ardent, but passionate
only through a powerful and regulated intellect . . . facing unflinch-
ingly the demon of doubt which is inseparable from the spirit of
belief." Of all three it might be said that "he had the knowledge of
worldliness and the passion of asceticism, and in him the two are fused
into an individual whole." All are symbols to be recommended "to
those who doubt, but who have the mind to conceive, and the sensibility to feel, the disorder, the futility, the meaninglessness, the mystery of life and suffering, and who can only find peace through a
satisfaction of the whole being."

This still point of peace is variously symbolized throughout Eliot's
poetry, and the variety of the symbols may obscure the connection between Eliot's image of the "rose-garden" and Becket. The "rose-garden," as Mr. Unger explains in his study of this image,[1] represents in
Eliot a moment of contact with reality, a moment of rare consciousness
and "sudden illumination," which flashes across the drab flux of ordinary life as the only meaningful moment (or moments) of that life—
an experience which the individual may try constantly and unsuccess-
fully to recapture. It is, in short, the "still point" in the life of the
individual. . . .

But the desire for this still point where all desires end is the saving
grace; the unredeemable or unconsummated moment in the worldly
garden is related to and indeed leads on to the Rose of Paradise, for the
object of desire is a moment of timeless reality, apprehended in the
world of time. The whole rose-garden scene of "Burnt Norton" suggests
the words of St. Bernard in Dante's Paradise: "That thou mayest con-

---

[1] Leonard Unger, "T. S. Eliot's Rose Garden: A Persistent Theme," *Southern
Review,* 7 (1942), 667–89.

summate thy journey perfectly . . . fly with thine eyes throughout this garden; for gazing on it will equip thy glance better to mount through the divine ray" (Canto xxxi). The religious implications of this imagery are enhanced by the echoes of St. Augustine's *Confessions* which, I think, introduce and conclude the description of the rose-garden in "Burnt Norton." Recall Eliot's meditation here on the theme that "Time past and time future . . . / Point to one end, which is always present"; recall that "Footfalls echo in the memory," that "My words echo / Thus, in your mind," leading to the evocation of the imagery of the rose-garden as a memory of a possible childhood experience. Then read Augustine's section on the problem of time (*Confessions,* Book XI), especially this passage:

> For if there be times past, and times to come; fain would I know where they be: which yet if I be not able to conceive, yet thus much I know that wheresoever they now be, they are not there future or past, but present. For if there also, future they be, then are they not there yet: if there also they be past, then are they not there still. Wheresoever therefore and whatsoever they be, they are not but as present. Although as for things past, whenever true stories are related, out of the memory are drawn not the things themselves which are past, but such words as being conceived by the images of those things, they, in their passing through our senses, have as their footsteps, left imprinted in our minds. For example, mine own childhood, which at this instant is not . . . but as for the image of it, when I call that to mind, and tell of it, I do even in the present behold it, because it is still in my memory. (Ch. XVIII, Loeb Library trans.)

Indeed, in this book of the *Confessions* (Ch. XI) Augustine expresses the central question of Eliot's later poetry:

> Who will hold [the heart of man], and so fix it, that it may stand a while, and a little catch at a beam of light from that ever-fixed eternity, to compare it with the times which are never fixed, that he may thereby perceive how there is no comparison between them . . . and that all both past and to come, is made up, and flows out of that which is always present? Who now shall so hold fast this heart of man, that it may stand, and see, how that eternity ever still standing, gives the word of command to the times past or to come, itself being neither past nor to come? Can my hand do this, or can the hand of my mouth by speech, bring about so important a business?

The difficulty is that the search for the still point involves the grasping of so many false points—a confusion represented in the *Coriolan* poems, which are closely related to *Murder in the Cathedral.* In "Triumphal March" the crowd is seeking desperately for "light," for a still point in the meaningless flux of life without faith, where the Sanctus

bell announces only "crumpets." As they watch the parade of death
and daily banality, they find the supreme moment, mistakenly, in their
glimpse of the worldly Leader. The terror of clinging to such a "point"
is displayed in "Difficulties of a Statesman," where the Leader, lost in
the flux of worldly affairs, is himself desperately searching for "a still
moment, repose of noon." Becket's career, as presented in the play,
provides the best commentary on *Coriolan.* The still point of peace for
which all cry is not of this world, though it may be glimpsed in this
world, as Becket's Christmas sermon shows: "He gave to His disciples
peace, but not peace as the world gives."

To this theme of the timeless reality glimpsed in the world of time
Eliot returns again and again in *Four Quartets,* with constant parallels
to *Murder in the Cathedral.* Thus, in "The Dry Salvages":

> Men's curiosity searches past and future
> And clings to that dimension. But to apprehend
> The point of intersection of the timeless
> With time, is an occupation for the saint—
> No occupation either, but something given
> And taken, in a lifetime's death in love,
> Ardour and selflessness and self-surrender.
> For most of us, there is only the unattended
> Moment, the moment in and out of time,
> The distraction fit, lost in a shaft of sunlight. . . .

Among the saints who are thus prepared to recognize the moment when
it comes are Augustine, Becket, Pascal, and the devotees of Little
Gidding; the Chorus of the play represents "most of us," unable to
anticipate, to understand, or to arrest the timeless moment.

The death of Becket, then, is one of these moments of illumination,
equivalent to a moment in the rose-garden: a parallel enforced by
Eliot's use of an identical sentence after the illumination in both
"Burnt Norton" and *Murder in the Cathedral*: "Human kind cannot
bear very much reality."

> Dry the pool, dry concrete, brown edged,
> And the pool was filled with water out of sunlight,
> And the lotos rose, quietly, quietly,
> The surface glittered out of heart of light,
> And they were behind us, reflected in the pool.
> Then a cloud passed, and the pool was empty.
> Go, said the bird, for the leaves were full of children,
> Hidden excitedly, containing laughter.

> Go, go, go, said the bird: human kind
> Cannot bear very much reality.

The experience is at once real and illusory. It is real because it represents one of those rare moments when humanity recognizes its deep need for contact with the "heart of light"—the still point, the Word, Dante's "deep light." As in any mirage, the sight of water signifies an intense feeling of need. The vision, however, is illusory, because it can only be experienced through the insubstantial forms of "time." For average humanity this effect of illusion is necessary, since such a moment of perception is too intense to be borne for long:

> the enchainment of past and future
> Woven in the weakness of the changing body,
> Protects mankind from heaven and damnation
> Which flesh cannot endure.

For the saint, however, such a perception is neither unbearable nor illusory, since he understands the true significance of the earthly moment and sees the higher realm in which the need will be satisfied. Hence Becket is able to explain the torment of the Chorus in its great cry, "I have smelt them, the death-bringers," which ends with the recognition of deep guilt and of deep need for a mediator:

> I have consented, Lord Archbishop, have consented.
> Am torn away, subdued, violated,
> United to the spiritual flesh of nature,
> Mastered by the animal powers of spirit,
> Dominated by the lust of self-demolition,
> By the final utter uttermost death of spirit,
> By the final ecstasy of waste and shame,
> O Lord Archbishop, O Thomas Archbishop, forgive us,
> forgive us, pray for us that we may pray for you, out
> of our shame.

The agony of the Women here, as the sexual imagery shows, comes from recognizing the degradation of humanity into the animal; and the echo of Shakespeare's "The expense of spirit in a waste of shame" extends the horror. In suffering their Lord to die, they feel "torn away" from the source of light. Becket's answer is very close to "Burnt Norton":

> Peace, and be at peace with your thoughts and visions.
> These things had to come to you and you to accept them.
> This is your share of the eternal burden,

The perpetual glory. This is one moment,
But know that another
Shall pierce you with a sudden painful joy
When the figure of God's purpose is made complete.
You shall forget these things, toiling in the household,
You shall remember them, droning by the fire,
When age and forgetfulness sweeten memory
Only like a dream that has often been told
And often been changed in the telling. They will seem unreal.
Human kind cannot bear very much reality.

These passages in "Burnt Norton" and the play may seem far apart, since one relates to a vision of beauty and the other to a vision of ugliness. But the two visions lead to one end. Either is an escape from the world of Hollow Men, which, says Eliot in "Burnt Norton,"

. . . is a place of disaffection
Time before and time after
In a dim light: neither daylight
Investing form with lucid stillness
Turning shadow into transient beauty
With slow rotation suggesting permanence
Nor darkness to purify the soul
Emptying the sensual with deprivation
Cleansing affection from the temporal.

The "daylight" is equivalent to the moment in the rose-garden; the darkness is equivalent to that "Dark Night of the Soul" of St. John of the Cross, the religious purgation which has been well explained by Mr. Unger in relation to *Ash Wednesday* and "Burnt Norton," and by Mr. Sweeney in relation to "East Coker." [2] Both ways lead to reality and to salvation, though they appear to be moving in opposite directions ("the way up is the way down"). The way of the Dark Night leads down through a stage of utter disgust with the physical (as in the above chorus) and reaches at the bottom a state of vacancy, where sense and spirit alike are momentarily nullified—a low point from which one can only return upward to grace. It is this state which the Chorus describes in its final chant as "the loneliness of the night of God, the surrender required, the deprivation inflicted."

One may clarify the interrelation of these symbols by dividing them

[2] Leonard Unger, "Notes on *Ash Wednesday*," *Southern Review*, 4 (1939), 745–70; and the essay cited in footnote 1. James Johnson Sweeney, "East Coker: A Reading," *Southern Review*, 6 (1941), 771–91.

into three channels to reality. The average man has two approaches. The first is through the physical and sensuous: through the rose-garden and its related symbols of natural beauty, freshness, and fertility: the hyacinth girl, childish laughter, the bird's song. The second is the opposite way of the Dark Night. The third way, reserved for superior individuals, leads directly upward, "Light upon light, mounting the saint's stair," as Eliot says in "A Song for Simeon."

Hence Becket and the Chorus simultaneously achieve stillness at opposite poles: Becket in a vision of ultimate being, the Chorus in a vision of ultimate nullity:

> *Becket.* I have had a tremor of bliss, a wink of heaven, a whisper,
> And I would no longer be denied; all things
> Proceed to a joyful consummation.

> *Chorus.* Emptiness, absence, separation from God;
> The horror of the effortless journey, to the empty land
> Which is no land, only emptiness, absence, the Void,
> Where those who were men can no longer turn the mind
> To distraction, delusion, escape into dream, pretence,
> Where the soul is no longer deceived, for there are no objects,
>   no tones,
> No colours, no forms to distract, to divert the soul
> From seeing itself, foully united forever, nothing with
>   nothing. . . .

This experience of purgation is similar to that of *Ash Wednesday*. The Chorus is detached from the world to face a moment of reality, and the vision of utter destruction which it sees is really the road to exaltation. The passage just cited is the lowest point of the Chorus, although horror reaches greater intensity in the next chant, during the murder of Becket. In the latter the Women are really on the upward way, but, as usual, they misunderstand, "They know and do not know":

Clear the air! clean the sky! wash the wind! take stone from stone and wash them.
The land is foul, the water is foul, our beasts and ourselves defiled with blood.
A rain of blood has blinded my eyes. Where is England? where is Kent? where is Canterbury?
O far far far far in the past: and I wander in a land of barren boughs: if I break them, they bleed; I wander in a land of dry stones: if I touch them, they bleed.

The blood of Becket is purification, not defilement, for those who are contrite and ask for cleansing. The rain of blood is akin to Eliot's usual symbol of redemption, the water for which the Waste Land cries. And in this passage, together with suggestions of an Egyptian plague, of the land of Polydorus, of the stones leading to Dante's river of Blood, and of the bleeding boughs of the Suicides in the *Inferno* (Cantos xii and xiii), we have a specific echo of Eliot's own *Waste Land*: "And the dead tree gives no shelter, the cricket no relief, / And the dry stone no sound of water."

The Chorus, in fact, has begun the play in exactly the state described in the opening lines of *The Waste Land*: the state of those who fear a conscious life:

> Now I fear disturbance of the quiet seasons:
> Winter shall come bringing death from the sea,
> Ruinous spring shall beat at our doors,
> Root and shoot shall eat our eyes and our ears,
> Disastrous summer burn up the beds of our streams
> And the poor shall wait for another decaying October.

As in "Burnt Norton," these things are seen "in a shaft of sunlight," though the Chorus would avoid the illumination, "living and partly living"—living, that is, an animal existence, not the full life of conscious humanity. Salvation comes through the gradual growth of consciousness and the acknowledgment of sin.

The choruses of the play thus echo and prophesy the whole development of Eliot's poetry. The chorus opening Part II, which was substituted in the second edition of the play for the ecclesiastical procession of the original version, is closely related to the garden scene of "Burnt Norton," to "A Song for Simeon," to "Marina," to the *Landscapes,* "New Hampshire," "Rannoch," and "Cape Ann," and, in its imagery of the bird's song amid barrenness, to the many other places where Eliot uses this imagery of desired fertility and rebirth. This revision seems to me an improvement over the original Biblical chants, partly because it strengthens the play's unity by showing the effect of Becket's sermon on the Chorus, which here no longer fears the coming of Spring; and also because the revision is closer to the heart of Eliot's poetry and thus draws strength, as do the other choruses, from connection with the body of the poet's work.

To illustrate these relations fully, I should like to concentrate upon the difficult chorus already cited, that of "the death-bringers." Readers have disagreed widely in the evaluation of this, some placing it among "the greatest poetry of our day," others declaring that its "force is just violence, not really poetic force." Misunderstanding and dissatisfaction arise from viewing this chorus as simply "a prescience of evil"; it is certainly this, but not simply this. Eliot is creating here the vision of a universe without order, a vision given in the only way in which the "type of the common man" can realize it, by all the "quickened senses." The order of time is abolished: the merry fluting of a summer afternoon is heard at night mingled with the owl's "hollow note of death." Bats, with the huge scaly wings of Lucifer, slant over the noon sky. The creative mind of God and Man is gone; the scavengers and the least sensitive, least conscious forms of life take over. The threat of death exists even in the most delicate flowers. And with this disorder humanity feels its involvement: "I have lain on the floor of the sea and breathed with the breathing of the sea-anemone, swallowed with ingurgitation of the sponge." But, paradoxically, the Women are saved, not lost, by such a vision, for here gradually emerges the human consciousness at highest intensity, recognizing all creation as part of a pattern which points to this moment, seeing themselves as "death-bringers," admitting sin, crying for absolution. The disorder in the first two-thirds of this chorus, with its long, irresolute lines, changes to a balanced order of versification, phrasing, and thought as the Chorus recognizes its responsibility:

> Have I not known, not known
> What was coming to be? It was here, in the kitchen, in the passage,
> In the mews in the barn in the byre in the market place
> In our veins our bowels our skulls as well
> As well as in the plottings of potentates
> As well as in the consultations of powers.

Comparison with *The Waste Land* and "The Dry Salvages" shows this chorus as central to the body of Eliot's poetry. Here is "What the Thunder Said": the "Murmur of maternal lamentation," the vision of the dissolution of human order and history, which lead to the Chapel Perilous and the "damp gust / Bringing rain." The opening of "The Dry Salvages" creates much the same feeling of the dissolution of human order and human time. Here the river is a "death-bringer," always involved with man, however remote it may appear. The rhythm, the time kept by the river is equated with the natural flow of man's life from birth to death, as Miss Gardner has said.[3] Miss Gardner has also shown that the movement of the river differs from that of the sea,

---

[3] Helen Gardner, "Four Quartets: A Commentary," in *T. S. Eliot: A Study of His Writings by Several Hands,* ed. B. Rajan (London, Dennis Dobson, 1947), pp. 57–77; see esp. pp. 67–8.

which is without direction; and this is a crucial distinction in understanding the poem. If man looks beyond the rhythm of his own machines, he can understand the river's movement from source to mouth, which is like the movement from past to future; but when the river, the "brown god," merges with the sea, which contains "Many gods and many voices," man's sense of direction and of time is lost:

> The tolling bell
> Measures time not our time, rung by the unhurried
> Ground swell, a time
> Older than the time of chronometers, older
> Than time counted by anxious worried women
> Lying awake, calculating the future,
> Trying to unweave, unwind, unravel
> And piece together the past and the future. . . .

We watch with wonder the sea and

> Its hints of earlier and other creation:
> The starfish, the hermit crab, the whale's backbone;
> The pools where it offers to our curiosity
> The more delicate algae and the sea anemone.

Here the relation of this *Quartet* to the play becomes clear. The "anxious worried women" are like the Chorus of Women of Canterbury who are attempting to measure events on a human scale, but are dragged, as by the bell tolling with the ground swell, to a bewildering vision of a universe which will not fit into the human order, to a terrifying sense of some relation with the "living things under sea," and finally to a sense of design, not that of past and future, but a design centered upon a timeless moment of illumination, a still point round which the world is ordered: the death of God's martyr, an "instant eternity." The bell of "The Dry Salvages" indicates such a moment, giving significance to a life of which we can otherwise only say, "There is no end, but addition: the trailing / Consequence of further days and hours." The bell, like the death of Becket, is "perpetual angelus," a remembrance of the Incarnation. Through its "symbol perfected in death," the play presents the "end" of man envisaged in "Burnt Norton":

> The inner freedom from the practical desire,
> The release from action and suffering, release from the inner
> And the outer compulsion, yet surrounded
> By a grace of sense, a white light still and moving. . . .

Murder in the Cathedral:
The Theological Scene

by Francis Fergusson

You know and do not know, what it is to act or suffer.
You know and do not know, that acting is suffering,
And suffering action. Neither does the actor suffer
Nor the patient act. But both are fixed
In an eternal action, an eternal patience
To which all must consent that it may be willed
And which all must suffer that they may will it,
That the pattern may subsist, that the wheel may turn and still
Be forever still.

—Thomas to the Women of Canterbury, and the
Fourth Tempter to Thomas

Murder in the Cathedral, considered simply as a modern play, owes
a great deal to continental theater-poetry, which I have sampled in the
work of Pirandello, Cocteau, and Obey. It is most closely akin, in its
dramaturgy and its formal sense, to *The Infernal Machine*: it has a
similar coherence for the eye of the mind, a comparable esthetic intelli-
gibility. It may be regarded as a work of art in the same way. But it is
based upon a different idea of the theater; it seeks a different (and far
more radical) basis in reality. It was written for the Canterbury Festival, June 1935, and it takes the audience as officially Christian. On this
basis the play is a demonstration and expression of the "right reason"
for martyrdom and, behind that, of the right doctrine of human life
in general—orthodoxy. It is thus theology, a work of the intellect, as
the continental plays are not. *The Infernal Machine* and *Noah* represent myths; *Murder in the Cathedral* represents (by way of the story

From The Idea of a Theater: A Study of Ten Plays *by Francis Fergusson (Princeton, N.J.: Princeton University Press, 1949), pp. 210–22. Reprinted by permission of
Princeton University Press. Copyright 1949 by Princeton University Press.*

of Thomas à Becket) a type of *the* myth, the central, the basic myth of the whole culture. Only after its performance at the Canterbury Festival did it enjoy an after-life in the commercial theater in London, in our Federal Theater, and in the limbo of the academic theaters all over the world.

The continental plays came out of the theater, and Cocteau's phrase *poetry of the theater* applies to them accurately; but *Murder in the Cathedral* (in spite of its theatrical dexterity) did not. In this play Eliot is not so much a poet of the theater as a poet and theologian who uses the stage for his own purposes; and though he seems to have benefited from the Paris theater, he has no connection with any theatrical arts actually practiced in English. The play has some of the abstractness of *Everyman,* which Eliot has called the one play in English "within the limitations of art"; but he does not seek to reawaken this sense of drama, in the manner of Cocteau, for example, who with his "gloire classique," seeks to echo the not-quite-lost Baroque theatricality. In its conception, its thought, its considered invention of a whole idea of the theater, *Murder* is unique in our time; and it is therefore more important to investigate what kind of thing it is (and is not) than to reach any judgment of its ultimate value as drama.

The basic plot-structure appears to be derived from the ritual form of ancient tragedy. The first part corresponds to the agon. The chief characters are the Chorus of Women of Canterbury, three Priests, four Tempters, and Thomas. The issue—whether and how Thomas is to suffer martyrdom for the authority of the Church—is most explicitly set forth in the scenes between Thomas and the Tempters, while the Priests worry about the physical security of the Church, and the Women suffer their premonitions of violation, a more metaphysical horror. The First Tempter, a courtier, offers pleasure, "kissing-time below the stairs." The Second, a Royalist politician, offers secular power, "rule for the good of the better cause." The Third, a baron, offers the snobbish comfort of acceptance by the best people, the security of the homogeneous class or tribe. These three echo motivations from Thomas's past, which he has completely transcended, and can now dismiss as "a cheat and a disappointment." But the Fourth Tempter offers Thomas the same formula ("You know and do not know, what it is to act or suffer") which Thomas had himself offered the Women when he first appeared; and he shows Thomas that his acted-suffered progress toward martyrdom is motivated by pride and aims at "general grasp of spiritual power." For the first time, Thomas nearly despairs: "Is there no way, in my soul's sickness / Does not lead to damnation in pride?" he asks. There follows a chorus in four parts, triumphant

Tempters, Priests, and Women, envisaging and suffering Thomas's danger in their various ways; after which Thomas sees his way clear, the "right reason" for suffering martyrdom. This is the climax and peripety of Thomas's drama and the dramatic center of the play; and I shall consider it in more detail below. It concludes the first part.

There follows an Interlude: Thomas's Christmas sermon addressed directly to the audience. He sets forth the timeless theory of the paradox of martyrdom: mourning and rejoicing, living and dying in one: the bloody seed of the Church. From the point of view of the dramatic form, it corresponds to the epiphany following the agon and the choral pathos of Part I. It is also another demonstration, in another mode of discourse and another theatrical convention (the sermon), of the basic idea of the play.

Part II is, from the point of view of Thomas's drama, merely the overt result, the more extended pathos and epiphany, of his agon with the Tempters: he merely suffers (and the audience sees in more literal terms) what he had foreseen at the end of Part I. This part of the play is in broad, spectacular effects of various kinds. First there is the procession of the Priests with banners commemorating three saints' days: those of St. Stephen, St. John the Apostle, and the Holy Innocents. The four Knights (who replace the Tempters of Part I and, as a group, correspond to them) come to demand that Thomas yield to the King, and then they kill and sanctify him at once. The killing is enacted in several steps, including a chorus in English (one of the best in the play) while the Dies Irae is sung off-stage in Latin. After the killing the Knights advance to the front of the stage and rationalize the murder in the best British common sense political style. The immediate effect of the Knights is farcical—but, if one is following the successive illustrations of the idea of the play, their rationalization immediately fits as another instance of wrong reason. If it is farce, it is like the farce of the Porter in *Macbeth*: it embodies another aspect of the subject of the play. Part II as a whole, corresponding to a Shakespearean last act and to the catastrophe with chorus and visual effects at the end of a Greek tragedy, is rhythmic, visual, exciting, and musical—contrasting with Part I which is addressed essentially to the understanding.

Though the form of the play is derived from ritual tragedy, it is far more abstractly understood than any traditional ritual tragedy. It is based not only upon Dionysian but also upon Christian ritual, and upon the resemblance between them. The human scene, or social focus, is generalized in the same way: the Cathedral is neither Canterbury in 1935 nor Canterbury in 1170 but a scheme referring to both, and also to a social order like that which Sophoclean tragedy reflects; a three-part order consisting of the people, individuals with responsible roles in church or state, and the shepherd of the flock who is responsible for the tribal religion. Hence the dramatis personae are, in their initial conception, not so much real individuals as roles in the life of the schematic community: there are resemblances between Knights and Tempters, and between both and the Priests, which deprive all of them of complete individuality and point to ideas which the stage figures represent. The peculiar qualities of the play—its great intellectual scope and distinction as well as its allegorical dramatic style—rest upon the abstractness of its basic conception, so unlike that of ritual drama in a living tradition. The best place to study the scheme, or the dramatic machinery of the play, is Thomas's peripety at the end of Part I.

The ways which Eliot finds to represent Thomas at the crucial moment of his career are entirely unlike those by which Obey presents his Noah. Obey makes-believe Noah as a real man and "God's world" as real. He then shows Noah living moment by moment, in the alternation of light and darkness, and in the palpable effort to obey his *Deus Absconditus*: he appeals to our direct perception and to analogies in our own experience. Eliot does not seek to grasp Thomas imaginatively as a person; he rather postulates such a man, and places him, not in God's world but in a theological scheme. He then indicates both the man and his real, i.e., theological, situation indirectly by means of the significant elements which he assembles: Tempters, Priests, and Chorus of Women.

The first three Tempters do not tempt Thomas, because he is completely beyond the temptations they offer. They set forth three forms of temptation which are not so much realized in human character as expressed in the varied music and imagery of their verse. The Fourth Tempter does not really tempt Thomas either: he reveals a temptation to which Thomas is in danger of succumbing; but as soon as Thomas sees it, it ceases to be a temptation and becomes the instrument of purgatorial suffering. From this suffering come Thomas's desperate questions or appeals, ending with "Can I neither act nor suffer / Without perdition?" To which the Fourth Tempter replies with the action-passion paradox which I have quoted. There follows a choral passage in four parts which, in its development, resembles what Thomas must be undergoing. The four Tempters chant their triumphant despair: "Man's life is a cheat and a disappointment." The Priests utter their very secular fright: "Should we not wait for the sea to subside?" The Chorus, the Priests, and the Tempters in alternation present a vision of horror: "Death has a hundred hands and walks by a thousand ways." The Chorus then appeals to Thomas: "God gave us always some reason, some hope," they chant, "but now a new terror has soiled us"; and the passage concludes,

"O Thomas Archbishop, save us, save us, save yourself
that we may be saved;
Destroy yourself and we are destroyed."

To which Thomas answers (though, it seems, not directly to the Chorus):

"Now is my way clear, now is the meaning plain:
Temptation shall not come in this kind again.
The last temptation is the greatest treason:
To do the right deed for the wrong reason."

He then thinks over his career as he now sees it: his deluded pursuit of worldly triumphs, pleasures, and powers—talking to himself or the audience rather than to any of the figures on stage.

The difficulty of this passage is in grasping Thomas's peripety (or conversion) dramatically; and this is a matter both of the action Eliot is imitating and of the means he uses.

The chief means is the four-part chorus. *Murder* is the only modern play in which the chorus is an essential part of the dramatic scheme, and here the chorus plays a role similar in several respects to that of the Sophoclean chorus: i.e., it expresses, in the music and imagery of verse, if not what Thomas suffers, at least the suffering (depraved or painful) which results from Thomas's peril—a suffering similar to his yet on a completely different level of awareness, as the suffering of the Sophoclean chorus, in its real but mysterious world, is not. This chorus also reveals to Thomas the "right reason" (charity) for his martyrdom; but here again it does so without understanding anything itself, whereas the Sophoclean chorus, dim though its awareness is, to some degree shares a sense of the final good of all. We must suppose that Thomas hears their chanted appeal, and sees thereby the will of God (as distinguished from his own ambitious or suicidal will) in his progress toward martyrdom. Thus Eliot has arranged the elements of his composition in such a way that we may (like Thomas himself) deduce both his change of heart and his right reason at this point—but we may do so only in the light of the orthodox doctrine, the theological idea, of martyrdom.

But Eliot carefully does not show this change in Thomas himself at this point. If we attempt to imagine him as a real man in a real situation—as an actor would be impelled to do if he were trying to act the role—we may either say that he has found a new and better rationaliza-

tion for the same deathly and power-mad impulse which drove him
before, and thus achieved simply another intellectual feat, or else that
the sudden intervention of Grace has removed him to a realm which is
completely invisible to us. For Thomas himself remains invisible: he
gives nothing, except the very interesting summary of his past and dead
worldly career as the Tempters revealed it to him. Later—in the Christmas sermon—he will give his reasons at length and in very general
terms; and after that, his life.

Before considering the allegorical dramaturgy and the peculiar
theology underlying this passage, it should be pointed out that it cannot be understood apart from the whole play, which is all a demonstration and expression of Thomas and his sanctification. The sermon
explains it, and Part II of the play shows it in comparatively realistic
terms. I have said that Part I corresponds to the agon; and it does
certainly complete Thomas's own drama: "I shall no longer act or
suffer, to the sword's end," he says at the end of it. But if one thinks of
the "drama" as the actual dispute with the drunken Knights, followed
by the real killing, then Part I may be considered a "Prolog im Him-
mel" which establishes the theological scene; and on this view its very
abstract style is easy to justify. But the theological scene is presented
as the sole reality; and in the realistic horrors of Part II everything moves
by its machinery—the drunken evil of the killers, the reflex fluttering
of the Priests, the abandoned and Wagnerian somnambulism of the
Chorus, and even Thomas, who goes through the motions without conviction, or rather with a conviction which is not literally represented
at all:

> "It is out of time that my decision is taken
> If you call that decision
> To which my whole being gives entire consent.
> I give my life
> To the Law of God above the Law of Man.
> Those who do not the same
> How should they know what I do?"

as he puts it to the totally uncomprehending Priests. Realistic though
Part II is, in a way, its reality is at the same time denied; and it is com-
posed according to the same formal principle, and in illustration of the
same idea, as Part I.

The purpose, or final cause, of the play is the demonstration of a
particular theological idea which one must attempt to grasp if the play
is to be understood. Mr. Eliot wrote of Pascal, in his introduction to
the *Pensées*: "Capital, for instance, is his analysis of the *three orders:*

the order of nature, the order of mind, and the order of charity. These three are *discontinuous;* the higher is not implicit in the lower as in an evolutionary doctrine it would be. In this distinction Pascal offers much about which the modern world would do well to think." This notion throws a good deal of light upon the schematic scene of *Murder in the Cathedral.* The Chorus would be in the order of nature; the Tempters, Priests and Knights in the order of the mind; and Thomas in the order of charity. Only the first two orders are visible to us, unless by Grace; but it is only in the order of Charity that Thomas and the form and meaning of the whole are finally intelligible. In the play, this order is represented by the doctrine which Thomas expounds in the sermon, and also by the abstract scheme of the play: the "three orders" and the three parts of society. Hence the mechanical feel of the play as a whole: the dramatis personae are as discontinuous from each other and from any common world as the parts of a machine, but they move according to the will of God as that is represented by (and deducible from) the theological doctrine. It is an idea of the divine plan, and of human experience as subject to it, which comes out of modern ideal-ism: one is reminded of Leibniz's preestablished harmony. Is this the way in which we must now understand Christianity? I do not know. And I do not assume that Mr. Eliot himself would say so. But it is the doctrine which this play demonstrates; and in the play, therefore, the whole realm of experience represented by the *Purgatorio,* the direct sense of moral change (not to be confused with evolution), of natural faith, and of analogies which make the three orders not completely dis-continuous—in short, the whole appeal to a real world which all may in some sense perceive—is lacking.[1]

On this basis one must understand the paradoxical notion of action which the play presents, and thence its dramatic form. The formal cause of the play (the clue to the plot, to the use of the stage, to the characterization, and to the verbal medium) is the idea of action expressed in the formula, "You know *and do not know* that acting is suffering / And suffering action."

In the play this formula works as a governing formal idea; but to avoid misunderstanding it is necessary to point out that this idea is it-self poetic, and derived from experience—from that direct sense of human life which I have been calling histrionic. The histrionic basis of Eliot's verse has often been pointed out; it is the source of its unique and surprising vitality. He is a metaphysical poet by instinct; he imi-

[1] The reader is referred to *The Idea of a Theater,* Chapter I, Part I, "Analogues of the Tragic Rhythm" and to Chapter II, Part I, "The Theater of Reason in its Time and Place," where this view of the *Purgatorio* is somewhat elaborated.

tates action by the music and imagery of his verse, or he defines it, or he does both at once:

> "The child's hand, automatic . . ."

> "My friend, blood shaking my heart,
> The awful daring of a moment's surrender . . ."

> "The lost heart quickens and rejoices
> At the lost lilac and the lost sea voices . . ."

The action-suffering formula may be regarded as an achievement, in the medium of metaphysical poetry, for which all of Eliot's work up to that time had been a preparation. But part of this preparation must have been the study of the great dramas of the tradition; and the best way to grasp the scope of the formula is to compare it with the notions of action in three landmarks which I have studied: the tragic rhythm of Sophocles, the rational action of Racine, and the passionate action of Wagner.

The Sophoclean tragic rhythm spreads before us, in time, a spectrum of modes of action, from reasoned purpose, through suffering informed by faith, to a new perception of the human creature: the moment of the "epiphany." The whole movement occurs in time; and when, at the end of a figure, we see the human creature in a new light, it is still the human creature that we see, in a world continuous (by analogy) with that of common sense. It is only by means of this tragic rhythm repeated in varied figures that the action of the play as a whole is conveyed, also by analogy: and what is conveyed is not a verbal formulation but an action which we are invited to apprehend sympathetically and histrionically. Eliot's action-suffering formula is a generalization derived from the tragic rhythm; and it seeks to fix human action (beneath the "masquerades which time resumes") as it timelessly *is* in the hand of God. The tragic rhythm as such disappears when thus abstractly considered; and the elements of Eliot's composition are regarded not as imitations of the one action but as illustrations of the one eternal formula.

In this respect *Murder in the Cathedral* is closely akin to the "ideal" dramas of Racine and Wagner, which celebrate respectively action as rational, and action as passion (or suffering). The action-suffering paradox comprehends the complementariness of reasoned purpose and mindless passion which I endeavored to point out in Chapter IV, when considering Racine and Wagner. But though the notion of action in

Murder seeks to comprehend and transcend Racine's and Wagner's visions, it implies, like them, the univocal sense of form and the idealist principles of composition. Thus the ideal perfection of the chorus is due to the fact that it exists primarily (like *Tristan*) as the expression, in music and imagery, of a mode of suffering, and only secondarily as "The Women of Canterbury": the performers would make it come alive by understanding the music rather than by understanding poor old women. And so for the Priests, Tempters, and Knights: they are demonstrations, and expressions in imagery, of rationalizations first, and men second, as though by an afterthought. The dramatis personae (essences of discontinuous worlds of experience) have nothing in common but the blank and meaningless fact of the killing—except Thomas. He knows what he act-suffers as the rest do not. The "basis in reality," which Mr. Eliot says every convention must have, is in Thomas's invisible moment of illumination, "the occupation of a saint." Thus a unique relation between author, performers, and audience is established: they are as discontinuous (and "perfect") as the dramatis personae. The perfection of the choral music, the elegance of the reasoned demonstrations by Tempters, or Priests, or by Thomas in his sermon, is gained by accepting completely the limitations of a super-idealist convention. Hence the nightmarish feel of the play: all is explicit and expressed, yet all moves by unseen machinery and speaks by ventriloquism. This sense of dramatic form is akin both to the "despotic ideal" which Baudelaire felt in Wagner's orchestration, and to the a priori and almost actor-proof perfection of the Racinian Alexandrines.

If one considers, not the perfection of the discontinuous parts of the play but the perfection of the whole, it appears that all the parts are instances of the action-suffering, knowing-unknowing formula. It is in this way that the play as a whole coheres in the eye of the mind: the general scheme has the beauty of the perfectly formed and aptly illustrated thought. In Mr. Eliot's three orders, the realm of the mind would appear to be in some sense higher than that of nature, where his Chorus suffers in complete mindlessness. And he seems to have proposed to himself a dramaturgic problem like that which Corneille tackled in *Polyeucte,* and Cocteau in *The Infernal Machine*: to show, in the mirror of reason, a change of heart. He might have taken as his motto and principle of composition Cocteau's suggestive remark, "Resemblance is an objective force which resists all the subjective transformations. Do not confuse resemblance with analogy." Thus the form of the play is most closely akin to the masterpieces of the Rationalist tradition.

But Mr. Eliot parts company with this tradition, even more radically

than Cocteau, by explicitly denying the reality of that "order of mind"
in which the art of the play is legible:

> "Those who do not the same,
> How should they know what I do?"

asks Thomas. To this question there can be no reply. The play does
not rest upon direct perception or natural faith; it does not base itself
upon analogies in common experience. It does not assume that reason
and the "mirror of reason" capture the truth of the human situation: it
rests upon revealed truth, which can only reach us here below in the
form of the paradoxical formulas of theology, at once reasoned and
beyond reason. From the concepts of theology all is deduced: the very
idea of a theater as well as the clue to the form of the play and the selection of illustrations. One might put it that the purpose, or final cause,
of the play, which distinguishes it from any other drama, is precisely
to demonstrate and express the priority, the sole reality, of this same
final cause.

But, while recognizing the unique purpose of the play, I wish to
study its formal rather than its final cause: to consider it as drama
rather than theology. And I wish to offer two observations upon it as an
example of the art of imitating action.

The first is that, whatever one may think of its theology and its
epistemology, it cannot be dismissed as simply "unreal." It almost
completely eschews photographic or modern realism; but the sense of
human action which it conveys is very much like that which we get
from other first-rate modern drama with a strong intellectual and ethi-
cal motivation, Ibsen's and Pirandello's for example. If one learns to
understand the extremely consistent conventions of *Murder in the
Cathedral,* one may read it as an imitation of that human action which
we know from a thousand other sources: human life divided by the
machinery of the mind, and confined by the greedy idolatries of the
sensibility. The theological "basis in reality" which Eliot accepts may
be regarded as an interpretation reached inductively through this common experience, even though Eliot presents it as the truth from which
all is deduced.

The second observation follows from the first: in spite of its absolute
finality and its ideal perfection, *Murder in the Cathedral* should be
regarded as employing only one of many possible strategies for making
modern poetic drama—which is as much as to say that the problem
has not been solved in the sense of Sophoclean or Shakespearean drama.
Mr. Eliot himself has explored other modes of action and awareness,
other, less idealized relationships between poet and audience, both in

his verse and in his other plays. I have quoted some of the explicit imitations of action to be found in his verse. In *The Rock,* the reality of time and place, of the historic moment, is explored as it is not in *Murder in the Cathedral.* In *Family Reunion* Mr. Eliot seems to be seeking a more realist type of dramaturgy; and he seeks it (like Obey in *Noah*) in the complex and prerational relationships of the Family. In short, Mr. Eliot's own practice in his other works invites us to consider *Murder in the Cathedral,* in spite of its perfectionism, not as the drama to end all dramas but as one example of the art in our confusing times.

Hence the purpose of placing it in relation to Cocteau's and Obey's poetries of the theater. As imitations of action, the three plays are comparable; three attempts to bring the light of the tradition to bear upon the contemporary human; three partial perspectives of great value and suggestiveness. A contemporary idea of the theater, if we had it, would leave room for them all as well as for some of the values of modern realism which modern poetry of the theater, or in the theater, has to do without.

Action and Suffering:
Murder in the Cathedral

by Grover Smith

For the Canterbury Festival of June, 1935, Eliot wrote his first independent full-length drama, *Murder in the Cathedral*.[1] Though, unlike
The Rock, this play was a product of his own architectonic, it was not
originally an independent venture into the competitive world of the
theater. Assured of an audience to whom for the occasion the subject
would appeal, Eliot was again able to indulge his affection for religious
symbolism without calculating, as was needful with his later plays, the
odds against success if he did not compromise with the public caprice.
He could remain a poet writing about life on his own terms without
unduly fretting over the fact that these were not the terms of most
other people. *Murder in the Cathedral,* in other words, is just as much
coterie literature as Eliot's earlier poetry. It has had a good deal of
vogue among audiences possessing religious sympathies; and it enjoyed
a good London run at the small Mercury Theatre, at the Duchess Theatre in the West End, and at the Old Vic, to which it returned in 1953.
It has been a favorite with amateur companies, and on both sides of
the Atlantic it has often been produced by university undergraduates.

---

[1] Critical appraisals are numerous; among the most useful are Francis Fergusson,
The Idea of a Theatre (Princeton, N.J., 1949), pp. 210ff.; Theodore Spencer, "On
'Murder in the Cathedral,'" *Harvard Advocate,* CXXV, no. 3 (December, 1938),
21–22; Leo Shapiro, "The Medievalism of T. S. Eliot," *Poetry,* LVI (July, 1940),
202–13; D. S. Bland, "The Tragic Hero in Modern Literature," *Cambridge Journal,*
III (January, 1950), 214–23; Louis L. Martz, "The Wheel and the Point: Aspects of
Imagery and Theme in Eliot's Later Poetry," *T. S. Eliot: A Selected Critique,* ed.
Leonard Unger (New York and Toronto, 1948), 444–62; Grete and Hans Schaeder,
Ein Weg zu T. S. Eliot (Hameln, 1948), pp. 93ff.

An operatic version with a musical score by Ildebrando Pizzetti was staged in 1958. Made into a film, the play was given a *première* at Venice in 1951, but the venture achieved little popularity. The play is too static and difficult for the screen.

There are six published versions of *Murder in the Cathedral*; the abbreviated and complete versions of 1935; three revisions, appearing in 1936, 1937, and 1938; and the film edition of 1952. The second edition (1936), which is the latest stage text to have been issued in the United States, and the film edition are adequate for most critical purposes. The other versions omit some speeches; they reassign a good many which had overburdened the Fourth Knight, whose part Eliot wanted doubled with one of the Tempters'; and they simplify and otherwise improve the Knights' prose apologies and the Archbishop's sermon. Only the film version contains important new material; this is detailed and explained, in the 1952 edition, by George Hoellering, producer of the picture and collaborator with Eliot in the screen adaptation. Besides the original introits (near the beginning of Part II), supplanted by a chorus in the 1936 edition, the film includes a preliminary speech by Becket to the ecclesiastics of Canterbury; a new chorus; a prose trial scene, showing Becket confronting King Henry, and an address by the Prior to the people in the cathedral. And, at the end, instead of the verbose declarations by the four Knights, it has three briefer statements, the last emphatically communicating what Hoellering oddly alludes to as "the main point of the whole play"—that the Knights rather than Becket best represent the views of an audience content that "the pretensions of the Church" should be subordinate to "the welfare of the State." [2] (Significant as this announcement is, it seems less important than the example set by Becket in making his will compliant with God's.) Although the film production, partly because of the professional portrayal of Becket by Father John Groser and partly because of Eliot's reading of the invisible Fourth Tempter's lines, is, despite its inherent deficiencies of action, vastly superior to any conceivable stage presentation, still the text itself by its innovations and by its exclusion of the final speeches of the Priests is less satisfactory as a unified and completed drama. The following account is, therefore, based chiefly upon the widely circulated second American edition [New York, 1936].

Some of the cosmopolitan sophisticates at the Venice film *première* are said to have been disappointed when *Murder in the Cathedral* be-

[2] T. S. Eliot and George Hoellering, *The Film of Murder in the Cathedral* (New York, 1952), p. 14.

lied their expectation of a detective thriller. Their error was not much worse than one might have foreseen from the inappropriateness of the title which Mrs. E. Martin Browne originally suggested and Eliot adopted. The play, though certainly taking its theme from the murder of St. Thomas à Becket in 1170, is not about "murder in the cathedral" but about the spiritual state of a martyr facing death, the spiritual education of the poor women who are witnesses to his sacrifice, and the wilful opposition of secular to eternal power. If Eliot had called it, as he is reported to have meditated doing, *The Archbishop Murder Case,* the reference, though equally misleading, would have been less indefinite. (He seems to have had some difficulty with his choice, which superseded, according to Ashley Dukes, the tentative title *Fear[s] in the Way,*[3] a quotation from Ecclesiastes appearing also on one typescript draft of *The Family Reunion;* this has little to do, that one can see, with either play.) It is true that the historical personality of Becket gave the foundation to the plot. Eliot took a good deal of care to make the historical actions accord with the most trustworthy accounts by Becket's contemporaries, but, since the play concerns rather what happens through the man than what happens to him, such details are largely incidental—as is all the action properly so called—to verbal expressions of various attitudes. That is, Part I, establishing the context of the spiritual struggle by means of Becket's exchanges with characters who are projections of it—the Women of Canterbury, the Priests, and the Tempters—virtually lacks historical authenticity and in all but a few respects is simply a prologue to the historical action of Part II; yet it sets forth the whole of the psychological choice that the action is only to ratify. It presents the motif of suffering, through Becket's decision not to act; Part II presents the motif of action, through Becket's suffering the acts of others. The categories of action and suffering constitute the internal rationale of the drama.

The few historical facts which Part I incorporates are ordinary. The most interesting of these are Becket's secret longing for martyrdom and his political background, symbolized most effectively by the chess game accompanying, in the film, his dialogue with the First Tempter. In contrast, Part II reflects some precise study of the events immediately preceding the murder, as is evident from comparison of the play with the eyewitness narratives of Grim and others in E. A. Abbott's *St. Thomas of Canterbury.*[4] The scene in the cathedral is especially derivative. Historically Becket refused to have the door barred, exclaiming,

---

[3] Ashley Dukes, "T. S. Eliot in the Theatre," *T. S. Eliot: A Symposium,* ed. Richard March and Tambimuttu" (London, 1948), p. 113.
[4] E. A. Abbott, *St. Thomas of Canterbury* (London, 1898).

as an anonymous chronicler reported, "Absit ut ecclesiam Dei castellum faciamus." In the play the terror of his adherents, who see the Knights as little better than "maddened beasts," recalls his exclamation, according to another report, against the "canes interfectores," or, it may have been, "carnis interfectores." When Eliot's Knights enter brandishing their swords and bawling, "Come down Daniel to the lions' den," in the manner of Lindsay's "Daniel Jazz," they make a jocular acknowledgment of the martyr's triumph, even while degrading themselves to beasts. Becket's retort in the play, "It is the just man who / Like a bold lion, should be without fear," translates the Archbishop's actual words, a quotation from Proverbs, chapter 28, in the Vulgate. If one ignores certain liberties taken with the sequence of events, it was only in Becket's dying prayer that Eliot enlarged conspicuously upon the early chroniclers. What Becket apparently said was that he commended his soul and his cause to God and St. Mary, to the martyrs St. Denis and St. Elphege, and to the patron saints of [that] church— the last, of course, including St. Elphege. Eliot followed the priest Grim in omitting Elphege from the prayer and including him in Becket's sermon and concurred with still other authorities, possibly the wrong ones, in understanding by the saints all the saints of the Church; but he added gratuitously the names of John the Baptist and the apostles Peter and Paul. The two last were the patrons of the ancient abbey founded by St. Augustine of Canterbury.

Tennyson in *Becket* adopted the legend of a violent storm after the murder; Eliot gave the storm symbolic treatment through the Chorus' frantic cry beginning "Clean the air" and containing the words "A rain of blood has blinded my eyes." Along with the symbol of rain he introduced the image of bleeding boughs, taken from classical epic or from II Esdras 5.3: "And blood shall drop out of wood, and the stone shall give his voice, and the people shall be troubled." Afterward, in the last speech of the Third Priest, he availed himself of the tradition about the murderers' ultimate doom to exile, shipwreck, and death among the infidels. (That same speech owes a great deal to purely verbal sources. Opening with testimony to the enduring power of the Church, it continues, ironically paralleling Heywood's *Hercules Furens* ["Goe hurtles soules, whom mischiefe hath opprest"],[5] with a condemnation of the Knights that has sometimes been compared with the anathema in Baudelaire's "Femmes damnées: Delphine et Hippolyte," [6] though perhaps indebted rhetorically to the "axletree" passage in

---

[5] See T. S. Eliot, *Selected Essays 1917–1932* (New York, 1932), pp. 87–88.
[6] E.g., by Malcolm Cowley, "Afterthoughts on T. S. Eliot," *New Republic*, LXXXVII, No. 1120 (May 20, 1936), 49.

Chapman's *Bussy D'Ambois.* In its second half the speech unexpectedly
echoes the *Iphigenia in Tauris* as translated by Gilbert Murray.) [7]

Murder in the Cathedral surprises by two strong dissimilarities to
George Darley's and Tennyson's verse plays on Becket—by the quality
of its diction and by Eliot's novel and peculiarly unhistorical treatment of the protagonist's character. Instead of assuming the common
judgment of Becket as overweeningly arrogant, waging a battle of personal and ecclesiastical spleen with a foe hardly more impoverished in
spiritual attributes, Eliot depicts him as humbly submissive, accepting
death, not resisting it. Darley in his *Thomas à Becket* creates a proud
statesman, deceitful and greedy for dominion, a Machiavel who aspires
to rival the king and who, repeatedly occupied in blasting the ears of
his enemies, dies with a curse against his murderer: "Execrabilis esto!"
Tennyson shows the prelate eschewing self-aggrandizement and exalt-
ing the Church, yet, for all his nobility, dying only as a statesman in a
contest for power. Accordingly both emphasize the robust aspect of
Becket: Tennyson in *Becket* shows him defending himself; Darley has
him putting up a stout fight, after abusing Traci as a "vile reptile." Of
course, Darley's play is egregiously silly, but Tennyson's, more scrupu-
lously than *Murder in the Cathedral,* conforms to the estimate put by
secular history upon Becket's quarrel with Henry II. The difference in
Eliot arises from the abstraction of a two-sided conflict between princes
of the Church and the State into a one-sided assault by pride upon
sanctity. There is no doubt that Tennyson's hero has few marks of saintliness apart from fidelity to the rights of the Church; Eliot's, after quell-
ing his confusion of will, is devoted less to the Church than to God—
were divided allegiance possible. Eliot would have got into grave difficulties if he had made Becket rougher. Since in *Murder in the Cathedral* Becket speaks to the Knights sternly, without discourtesy or scuf-
fling, he retains dignity and escapes arrogance. In the long view it is
impossible to say that Eliot was wrong in his distortion, which may
have created a Becket more like the "real" one than his apparent conduct ever revealed, a hero more deserving of sympathy than even the

---

[7] Orestes has just arrived at the temple of Artemis; he laments:

> I slew my mother; I avenged
> My father at thy bidding; I have ranged
> A homeless world, hunted by shapes of pain,
> And circling trod in mine own steps again.

—and, almost immediately after, speaks lines apparently echoed in *The Family
Reunion* (New York, 1939), p. 29:

> . . . these miseries, wherein I reel
> Through Hellas, mad, lashed like a burning wheel.

protagonist of Aubrey de Vere's urbane dramatic poem *St. Thomas of Canterbury.*

Because the Archbishop triumphs morally over both the Tempters and the Knights, it may be preferable not to call Eliot's play a tragedy. It is true that a morally victorious catastrophe occurs in Milton's tragedy of Samson. *Murder in the Cathedral* presents, moreover, certain parallels (as Louis L. Martz also has noticed) to Sophocles' *Oedipus at Colonus,* the finest classic tragedy of reconciliation through death. But in both this and *Samson Agonistes* the problem of evil is not only universal but individual, through the particular flaw generating ruin. Granted that remission of guilt, as well as retribution, comes within the scope of tragedy, one would still be nearly right in designating *Murder in the Cathedral* a comedy. For the death of Becket, though it results obviously from human sin, does not result from the only flaw the play ascribes to him—his pride as a prospective martyr. This he surmounts in time to reconsider; then he consents to martyrdom again in order to obey what he sees as God's will. The best analogue to Eliot's plot is the "moral-quest" theme of the moral interludes or the tribulation theme of the Book of Job. Indeed, Eliot could have borrowed his four Tempters from Job as easily as from late fifteenth-century drama. However, Becket's suffering comes after the temptation, and it really constitutes also the reconciliation.

Murder in the Cathedral is a drama of such symbolic relationships that the ingredients of tragedy are all present, but apportioned—in fact, allegorically—among the different characters rather than confined to Becket himself. There is a moral flaw, original and particular sin; there is (in the external view) a catastrophe, affecting the victim destined to expiation; there is justification. The first is manifested in the suggestions of the Tempters, the will and act of the Knights, and the suffering of the Chorus; the second, the martyrdom, is executed upon the sufferer, Becket; the third is fulfilled in the damnation of the Knights, the potential salvation of the Chorus, and the exaltation of the saint. The late Theodore Spencer aptly pointed out that the characters live on different levels of moral refinement: that is, Becket, the Priests, the Chorus of Women of Canterbury, and the murderers have, on a descending scale, distinct ideas of reality, ranging from the acute spirituality of Becket to the depraved worldiness of the Knights.[8] The cumulation of these, with a distributive allotment of dramatic functions, makes up the total movement sometimes called "tragic." But as in an obsolete pictorial convention, rejuvenated by the cubists, of

---

[8] Spencer, *Harvard Advocate,* CXXV, No. 3, 21–22.

depicting successive temporal states on the same spatial canvas (Duchamp's "Nude Descending a Staircase"), the different functions here coexist: the Knights are sin, the Chorus is suffering, Becket is martyrdom. This is "tragedy" *sub specie aeternitatis,* as it may appear to God. Francis Fergusson, remarking this quality in the play, compares the levels to the discontinuous "orders" of Pascal, discussed by Eliot in his Introduction to the *Pensées.*[9] But they are more than these. And the levels create something as distinguishable from Sophoclean tragedy as is a Greek frieze from the procession or battle it represents. In its "spatial" treatment of character *Murder in the Cathedral* is as static as a Grecian urn: it belongs almost to a genre which is pre-tragic, the ritual drama of sin and redemption, where all the components of strain and antithesis are externalized, discrete. The internal conflicts of Becket and the Chorus are, as it were, microcosmical.

The plot of *Murder in the Cathedral* has, therefore, two aspects: one in which the characters are static types and another in which they are persons capable of development. At the end of Part I, after dismissing the perfunctory temptations of worldly pleasure, subservience to the king, and alliance with the barons, Becket rejects the lure of conscious glory in martyrdom. In the first aspect this act is only an intensification, a validation of his status as an appointed martyr. The audience, though aware of his pride, knows nothing of his temptation until it is presented, and by then he is ready to spurn it. In the second aspect his moral struggle teaches him the meaning of martyrdom as the perfection of will. In like manner the Chorus is to learn the meaning of suffering. Becket's initial desire is imperfect: from this he rises to a greater good. In discovering that his grandiose will to be martyred is sinful, he allows the wheel of fortune to bear him materially down and morally up. (The parallel with *King Lear* in some ways is informative; the important structural difference lies in Eliot's having adopted the "imminent-horror" type of discovery praised by Aristotle with reference to the *Iphigenia in Tauris.*) Without the discovery it would not be easy for the audience to look upon the Archbishop as a human being at all, much less to see him as a real historical figure. Part I is necessary because unless Becket vanquished the Tempters it would be inexplicable that by his death he could vanquish the Knights. His inward conflict in Part I presages the outward conflict of Part II, where for him and the Knights the tension exploits physical power, not psychology, and where only for the Chorus does it still animate a spiritual combat. This tension, as the Women experience it, corresponds to the

---

[9] Fergusson, *The Idea of a Theatre,* pp. 210ff.

Christian drama of fall and regeneration; Atonement is symbolized by Becket. As martyr in Part II, Becket is a type of Christ, who also suffered temptation before entering upon the drama of action through suffering; as Becket's human temptations to sin, the Tempters are the whispering Adversary; as sinners and sufferers, the Women of Canterbury are types of fallen Adam, enacting the inward strife in imitation of Becket, who enacts it in imitation of Christ; and as persecutors, the Knights are Satan going to and fro in the earth and walking up and down in it. Becket, like Christ, is tested, slain, and exalted, not for his sin but for other men's. It goes without saying that Becket's early biographers did not neglect the comparison, by no means unusual in saints' lives, between this martyr and the Savior. But, of course, Becket does not really atone for others' sin, even though his death serves as a memorial example whereby the Women of Canterbury come to accept their lot. Despite the theme of the ritual scapegoat, to read literal Atonement into the events of the play would be to lift it wholly to the allegorical level.[10]

The ritual motif, aligning *Murder in the Cathedral* with *The Rock* through verbal effects reminiscent of liturgy and with *The Waste Land* through the theme of death and rebirth, endows this play with a kind of secondary pattern like that mentioned by Eliot in his essay on Marston. But, besides being deliberately allegorical, the pattern also functions through the transcendent character of Becket, who seems to achieve awareness beyond earthly experience. In his order of reality he faces something which neither the other characters nor the audience understands. Unlike Sweeney in *Sweeney Agonistes* he is not merely saying ambiguous words: he is reacting to a vision. His certainty of election to martyrdom depends on no omen comprehensible to his followers but on an interior refinement worthy to be called communion. His language when he talks of action and suffering, of the still wheel which turns, is that of one whose very sensibility gains mysterious access. This may all be dramatic illusion, arising in some measure from cryptic phrasing; but it is successful. To be sure, one might complain that Becket is a little too remote even in his most commonplace lines. Eliot bars the audience from Becket's innermost self.

In *The Rock*, there is more than a suggestion that the Rock because he is the Church in its eternal aspect represents the "still point" of

---

[10] There is an abhorrent hypothesis, fostered by Margaret Alice Murray and developed in Hugh Ross Williamson's *The Arrow and the Sword* (London, 1947), that Becket died as the sacrifice in a witch cult of the Cathar heresy! See Maud Bodkin, *Studies of Type Images in Poetry, Religion, and Philosophy* (London, New York, and Toronto, 1951), pp. 131–35.

communion with God and that the Chorus is the "wheel" of human
active life in the world. So in *Murder in the Cathedral* Becket and the
Women of Canterbury (like Tiresias and the forms populating his
memory) typify the dualism of eternity and time, duration and flux,
spirit and flesh, action by suffering and suffering by action. Here Eliot
has uncovered a paradox: the sufferer suffers only because of the actions
of himself or others. The Fourth Tempter says to Becket what Becket
has already said about the Chorus:

> You know and do not know, what it is to act or suffer.
> You know and do not know, that acting is suffering,
> And suffering action. Neither does the agent suffer
> Nor the patient act. But both are fixed
> In an eternal action, an eternal patience
> To which all must consent that it may be willed
> And which all must suffer that they may will it,
> That the pattern may subsist, that the wheel may turn and still
> Be forever still.

What preserves this from utter self-contradiction is the statement
"Neither does the agent suffer / Nor the patient act"; for, though by a
shift of time the human agent may become the human sufferer, each
role is distinct. One meaning of the passage is that every cause predi-
cates an effect, and every effect a cause; they cannot occur independ-
ently. When Becket speaks to the Chorus he thinks of himself as the
actor, the source of will, and the Women as passive recipients of sor-
rows and benefits resulting from his choice of martyrdom. But when
the Fourth Tempter (almost his *Doppelgänger*) flings the same words
back in his teeth, Becket seems to realize that unless the sufferer refrains
from willing to suffer and thus from soiling his hands with his own
blood, he cannot be a true martyr. After nearly blundering, Becket
recognizes that not only the Women but he himself must be passive. He
must only consent to the divine will, so that he shall suffer and shall
become for suffering in others the involuntary agent. Both action and
suffering come from God as the unsuffering "first agent" or first cause
of action. Aristotle, in speaking of the nature of movement (analogous
to action), compares the good, toward which desire moves, and by
which it is moved, to the unmoved center which in a wheel imparts
motion to the rim: "For everything is moved by pushing and pulling.
Hence just as in the case of a wheel, so here there must be a point
which remains at rest, and from that point the movement must origi-

nate." [11] Thus in the *De Anima;* and in the treatise *De Generatione et Corruptione* he uses another image to describe action and passion (i.e., passivity) which Eliot in part duplicated—the image of the physician, the curative diet, and the patient. A "first agent" (the physician) acts, without being acted upon, through a "last agent" (food), which, being acted upon, in turn acts upon a passive object (the patient).[12] So God as "first agent" acts through prevenient grace upon Becket; and Becket, as patient, consents. In like manner, because in this synergy his consent involves will, he also acts, but only as a "last agent," to afflict the Women of Canterbury with further suffering, which, when they consent to it, becomes an agency in their salvation. The consenting agent as such does not suffer, and the patient as such does not act: the former because he consents and is an instrument, and the latter (the Chorus) because it permits or "suffers" the benefits of the cure.

Obviously between God and Becket there is another "final agent," the Knights. Eliot does not, in this part of the play, expatiate on their function. It is related by inference, however, to the paradox of action and suffering. They, by malice, are to will what, despite them, is to bring about justice. Eliot owed to Spinoza, perhaps, the seeds of his concern with the aspect of eternity which makes "All partial Evil, universal Good." He abandoned Spinoza, it is true, over the very issue that would confirm the influence, for he has had no commerce with Spinoza's monistic denial of evil or with Leibniz' "best of all possible worlds." By the time he was ready to use the idea of universal reparation, he was under the sway of St. Augustine and the mystics, whose acknowledgment that "all things," as St. Paul understood, "work together for good to them that love God" lifts no blame from sin even though that, too, produces good.[13] This paradox of good through sin is subjacent to the Knights' defiance of God. When Becket first supposes that he has the right to precipitate his suffering he is aware that "the wheel may turn and still / Be forever still"; by a deeper intuition he knows that the still wheel, as God beholds it, incorporates all the pattern of interlocking good and evil which men can only view as flux. Confident that his cause is right, Becket proposes to act so as to vindicate the Church by bringing good from the evil will of his foes. There is no deflecting him from this purpose by temptations which involve compromise. But what he has forgotten is what he himself is easily able to object against a lesser temptation, that only the fool "may think / He can turn the

---

[11] *De Anima* iii. 10 (trans. J. A. Smith).
[12] *De Generatione et Corruptione* i. 7. Cf. Plato *Theaetetus* 156–57.
[13] Rom. 8:28.

wheel on which he turns." By making his own will the mover of action and suffering in himself, the Knights, and the Chorus, he would be attempting precisely this—and failing. For on the turning wheel, good as often produces evil as evil produces good; only with God are these resolved, without losing their peculiar character, into the perfection that man aspires to. Only God's will can be the criterion of right or wrong action and suffering. In supplanting God's will with his own, in electing to be the center of the wheel without God, Becket would be inviting, on his own responsibility, whatever evils might ensue from his choice: he would be committing the Knights' sins of pride and murder.

Aghast, he exclaims: "Can I neither act nor suffer / Without perdition?" While the Chorus, the Tempters, and the Priests counsel him to avert action, he comes to his awakening.[14] The only way in which he can reach the stillness of the turning wheel is to yield to the mover, the point that is not himself. Those who act, all but God, and those who suffer are inescapably on the wheel; those who consent with the will of God are as God. Confessing that he has been about to "do the right deed for the wrong reason," to give a sinful turn to the wheel, he explains that this temptation sprang from his will for good. "Sin grows with doing good," he says, like Milton in *Areopagitica* ("Good and evil we know in the field of this world grow up together almost inseparably"). Only by extinction of self-will can he avoid the mortal sin of pride at his moment of sacrifice. Accordingly he is content that he "shall no longer act or suffer, to the sword's end," for God, not he, is the only agent through whom good can proceed from evil, and what God wills brings neither pain nor suffering to one who accedes to it as to a vocation. The martyr, freeing himself from the wheel, can assist the ultimate redemption of time. Henceforth he will not act, for God will act through him; he will not suffer, for God will empower him to consent. He has made a "decision," he says later, "To which my whole being gives entire consent," a decision taken "out of time." In his Christmas sermon he is able to affirm to his people: "A martyrdom is never the design of man; for the true martyr is he who has become the instrument of God, who has lost his will in the will of God, not lost it but found it, for he has found freedom in submission to God." His is the Dantean faith: "La sua volontate è nostra pace."

"Burnt Norton," published in 1936, confirms the impression that Eliot was particularly interested in Aristotelian philosophy at about the time he was writing *Murder in the Cathedral*. Although it is possible

---

[14] The last lines of the alternating speeches were apparently derived from the passage in Montaigne's *Apology for Raimond Sebond* beginning ". . . ce furieux monstre."

that some of this came to him through St. Thomas Aquinas, the direct influence of Aristotle is traceable to Eliot's early studies in both Aristotle and Leibniz. To the same early period one may ascribe the formulation of the "body-soul theme" which the youthful poems had only foreshadowed. Aristotle's hylomorphism may have been much in Eliot's awareness at that time.

The Chorus in *Murder in the Cathedral,* though ostensibly active in the toils of life, can only be passive under the oppression of the State and the agony of personal sorrow.

> For, us, the poor, there is no action,
> But only to wait and to witness.

But by consenting, as Becket himself consents, the women look ahead to an end of action and suffering. They occupy a circumference, so to speak, of which Becket is the center, for they rely on him as the source of the movement they participate in. When he is the point, they are the wheel, as he is the wheel when God is the point. It is their dramatic function to comment upon the events they witness. They fit the role of sufferers by being ordinary hard-working women with no pretense to power. They are like the crowds of people in *The Waste Land,* passively moved by what a Buddhist would call "Samsara," the wheel of life. Their direct antithesis, of course, is the quartet of Knights. Both the Knights and the Chorus, as human beings, are capable of action and suffering and both, in some senses of the words, exist by both conditions; but Eliot confined them to separate functions in their relation to Becket: he contrasted action with suffering—the masculine with the feminine, the violator with the violated, the beast with the prey. It is ironic that, being also upon the wheel, the Knights, too, should revolve round the Archbishop. Once Becket's will unites with God's, once he "conquers the beast" by submission, their sinful action, always contributory to the plan of God, proceeds from a mover who is the man Becket.

Through most of the drama the polarity of action and suffering finds correspondence in the imagery appertaining to the Knights and the Chorus. The principal examples are in the choruses themselves and in the speeches of the protagonist. Perhaps the most prominent imagery is zoölogical; it has two purposes, to characterize the murderers, in which application it joins with the imagery of sensation, and to associate the passive Chorus with unredeemed, elemental nature. But not less important is the imagery of nature in wider aspects—the cycles of day and night, summer and winter, spring and autumn; these identify the Chorus with the great turning wheel of creation and corruption,

growth and ruin. Thus, too, as one might expect from Eliot's usual de-
vices, there is an undercurrent of sexual imagery, so hidden as almost
to elude remark, but springing up at times in the choruses. In this the
antithesis between violence and passivity becomes one between male
and female. The Women see the intrusion of Becket's struggle as a
disturbance, a strain. They want to be let alone. They speak of "births,
deaths and marriages," of girls who "have disappeared / Unaccount-
ably, and some not able to," of "private terrors" and "secret fears."
Gradually, as Becket's destiny—their doom, as they regard it—becomes perspicuous, the terrors increase until in the last chorus of Part
I they have heightened their imagery to the point of speaking of
"oppression and torture," "extortion and violence," "Our labour taken
away from us, / Our sins made heavier upon us," "the young man
mutilated, / The torn girl trembling by the mill-stream." And at this
juncture they begin to name the beasts—leopard, bear, ape, hyena—
the "Lords of Hell."

As the play lengthens toward its denouement (after the opening
chorus of Part II, where the Women balance against the retrospective
autumnal imagery of the start of the play an imagery that looks to the
coming spring, still buried in winter) they reach the extremity of having to accept an overt embrace of the bestial. In the extraordinarily
moving passage just after Becket's first wrangle with the Knights, they
acknowledge that death has violated them through every sense—smell,
hearing, taste, touch, and sight—whereby they have known, almost in
the intimacy of beast with beast, the creatures of the earth and sea.
This sensation, this identification, finds unequivocally sexual language
when the Women succumb to "the shamed swoon / Of those consenting to the last humiliation," subdued, violated, mastered, "Dominated
by the lust of self-demolition . . . / By the final ecstasy of waste and
shame." The echo of Shakespeare's "waste of shame" is not needed
for its sexual reference. The Chorus, when it resumes, faces the dread
of being "foully united forever, nothing with nothing," of being no
longer human, of being cast out into the Void behind the Judgment.
Eliot objectified thus, in the most galvanic verse he has published, the
nature of human consent to the will of God. Between Becket's submission to the acts of his murderers and the anguish of the Women's resignation to the divine will, of which the Knights are sinful instruments,
this astounding imagery stands as a precise symbol of both. The passion of the Women comes later in Part I than the consent already or-
daining Becket's tribulation; here in Part II, however, their spasm of
suffering leaves him behind, and they have died in will before his blood
spouts under the sword.

As the murderers hack at Becket's skull, the Women chant a tormented prayer for cleansing, for purification from defilement. Recalling that they "did not wish anything to happen," they utter a cry of dread at the unimaginable "instant eternity of evil and wrong" by which they are soiled, "united to supernatural vermin,"

> It is not we alone, it is not the house, it is not the city that is defiled,
> But the world that is wholly foul.

Nature itself, as at the moment of Adam's fall in paradise, becomes contaminated by the Knights' re-enactment of primal sin. The world is in the spiritual Dark Night of despair. But to the Women Becket has spoken earlier of the reconciling joy that shall replace their pain:

> Peace, and be at peace with your thoughts and visions.
> These things had to come to you and you to accept them.
> This is your share of the eternal burden,
> The perpetual glory. This is one moment,
> But know that another
> Shall pierce you with a sudden painful joy
> When the figure of God's purpose is made complete.

The birth of peace is to follow the ravishment of will; a sword has pierced their hearts only that death may give life, as Becket knows it must. It is in obedience to his own words that the doors have been opened to the irruption of merciless force.

With the prospect of assured beatitude, recompense, redemption of time, the Women raise their voices once more at the end of the play in a "Te Deum" beyond resignation. They have learned that all things, and even their loss, are for the divine glory and that even in denial there is affirmation. Yet not only in "both the hunters and the hunted" is the glory manifested, but in both resides the guilt of primal sin: in those who act and in those who suffer. The song of praise, therefore, which has acclaimed the goodness of creatures that a little earlier would have symbolized bestiality, ends with a supplication for personal forgiveness. The Women assume the burden disclaimed by the Knights. This paradox—that the Knights should have affirmed by denying and that the Chorus should have denied by affirming—is but contributory to the more central paradox of the wheel turning and still. Now at the price of humility all is appeased and adjusted. Catharsis is complete.

This terminal chorus is conspicuously indebted to Anglican ritual, including perhaps the English "Gloria in excelsis" and the "Benedicite, omnia opera." More than some previous choric passages it recalls *The Rock*. Since Eliot's verse in *Murder in the Cathedral* is not so mis-

cellaneous as in *The Rock,* the feeling of structural orderliness is
greater for the play. Much of the poetry spoken by the Chorus has a
comparatively quick rhythm, despite the inevitable blurring of syl-
lables which group recitation would cause; in actual staging, however,
the lines are allotted to antiphonal voices. Because here the Chorus is
not only an observer but a participant, at least in the moral progres-
sion of the work, its verse is often little different from that assigned to
Becket. In the lecture "Poetry and Drama" (1950) Eliot explained
that in his search for a *"neutral"* style, neither too modern nor in the
wrong way archaic, he had "kept in mind the versification of *Everyman,* hoping that anything unusual in the sound of it would be on the
whole, advantageous." [15] The influence of *Everyman* is more obvious in
the verse than in the plot, although an image reported by the Chorus,
"Death, God's silent servant," is suggestive of God's "mighty messenger." Eliot's principal debt appears in the rhyming passages of the
Tempters' dialogues with Becket, where the sharp, irregularly assorted
stresses, four to the line, mimic skilfully the meter of the old play.
Going further, Eliot sometimes introduced alliteration. The four-beat
measure, one of Eliot's favorites in the other plays and in the *Quartets*
as well, he had already used in *Sweeney Agonistes.* After *Murder in the
Cathedral* he cultivated simplification, retaining few of the mechanical
barriers that here somewhat insulate the dialogue from ordinary speech.
For choric purposes, his verse tends to be more dactylic in the plays
than elsewhere. Obviously it is allied to Old and Middle English alliter-
ative verse. Once in a while it gives way to a longer or shorter line.
One of the most intelligible choric sections, to an audience straining
its ears in the far gallery, is that in three-beat verses beginning "We
do not wish anything to happen." Elsewhere Eliot got his measure by
simple plagiarism: the stychomythic exchange between Becket and the
Second Tempter came in part from Sir A. Conan Doyle's tale of Sherlock Holmes "The Musgrave Ritual." [16]

Over against the preponderantly metrical language of the play stand
the sermon, preached on the historical Becket's text, and the prose
speeches of the Knights, who, after the murder, step forth to harangue
the audience. Ever cautious, Eliot admits only that in these speeches he
may have been slightly influenced by Shaw's *Saint Joan;* it is hard to
see how there could be any doubt. The purpose of the speeches is dra-

---

[15] Eliot, *Atlantic Monthly,* CLXXXVII, No. 2, 34. [Quoted by permission of the
President and Fellows of Harvard College.]

[16] See my article, "T. S. Eliot and Sherlock Holmes," *Notes and Queries,* CXCIII
(October 2, 1948), 431–32. This source, which Eliot has since acknowledged, was first
noted, I think, by Elizabeth Jackson.

matically clear only in the film version. As Hoellering says in his Preface, in their earlier form they rather amuse the audience than shock it. The Fourth Knight's plea for "a verdict of Suicide while of Unsound Mind" causes all but the most attentive to forget that his predecessor has incriminated the audience itself by pointing out that modern society does not want the Church to be meddlesome and by showing how he and his confreres have made the audience' kind of world possible. Those who are not misled by the Fourth Knight into dismissing the quartet as mere zanies at this point will detect the acute sarcasm of the First Knight's concluding admonition "not to loiter in groups at street corners [or] provoke any public outbreak." The film version, hitting hard with the incrimination passage, is less subtle and, perhaps, too simple; but if this is a play to be watched and heard, not just read, the easier post-climax is preferable.

In any case, there is some danger lest this message should nullify the laboriously wrought thesis that the contest has been waged between brute power and resigned holiness, and suggest instead that, as in Tennyson, it has been fought merely between the State and the Church. Becket is superior to the latter sort of quarrel, which would suit the mentality of the Second Priest, who seems close in spirit to the Knights, just as the First Priest resembles the Women and the third Becket himself. The Second Priest typifies the potential moral strength of the Knights' immoral practicality. He is not bad; he is only unsaintly. If the conflict were up to him, he would use force when he did not need to lie low, and lie low when he could not use force. Although the Third Priest grasps the final meaning, he, in turn, does so as a spectator rather than as a participant like the Women. In the last analysis the struggle vindicates the Church, not as the priesthood represents it, but as the laity, the Women of Canterbury, reconstitute its purpose after Becket through humility has shown them the way. Through Becket the Church becomes the Women and ceases to be merely the Priests. Thus the Knights' addresses to the audience ought to make an appeal not just to those on the side of the self-willed State but also to those overprizing the temporal authority of the Church. By martyrdom Becket has shown that the power of the Church as well as that of the laity must, in the mystical sense, be negative. And the Women in their meager lives of action will compose a Church dedicated to humility. What *The Rock* communicates vaguely is here an illumination: that the suffering of the Witness and the action of the witnesses are one and the same thing.

Murder in the Cathedral:

The *Figura* as Mimetic Principle

by *William V. Spanos*

Taking their lead from T. S. Eliot's retrospective remarks in "Poetry and Drama" (1951) about the special nature of the aesthetic problems encountered in writing *Murder in the Cathedral*,[1] recent critics of the play have tended to minimize its relationship to his later commercial plays and its contribution to a revival of genuine public poetic drama. One must not, however, be misled by Eliot into dividing his early and late drama too sharply. In "Poetry and Drama," Eliot speaks of *Murder in the Cathedral* from the point of view of his later concern with the exigencies of verse in the drama of contemporary life. But the problem of verse represents only a special and advanced aspect of the broader, though more pressing problem to which Eliot has addressed himself from the beginning of his career as a dramatist, that is, the general problem of the levels of vocality in the action of the drama. Posed by the disintegration of modern culture and the consequent bifurcation of the dramatic sensibility, the problem is manifested in the impaired poetic potential of the two resulting types of drama: that of the naturalistic imagination, which achieves concrete reality at the expense of universality or value (the drama of the early Ibsen, for example) and that of what Allen Tate calls the "angelic imagination," [2] which achieves value at the expense of concrete reality (the drama of Maeterlinck, for example). Seen in these terms, *Murder in the Cathedral* is not,

"Murder in the Cathedral: *The* figura *as mimetic principle*," *by William V. Spanos. From* Drama Survey, *III, 2 (October, 1963), 206–23. Copyright 1963 by Drama Survey. Reprinted with alterations in* The Christian Tradition in Modern British Verse Drama *(New Brunswick, New Jersey: Rutgers University Press, 1967). Reprinted by permission of the author and* Drama Survey.

[1] *On Poetry and Poets* (London, 1957), p. 79.

[2] "The Symbolic Imagination," *The Man of Letters in the Modern World: Selected Essays, 1928–1955* (New York, 1955), p. 97: "I call that human imagination angelic which tries to circumvent the image in the illusory pursuit of essence. . . ."

as David E. Jones maintains, a "special case" incapable of supplying "a generally applicable formula," [3] nor, as Denis Donoghue claims, a reversion to nineteenth-century poetic drama.[4] It represents, rather, Eliot's first positive achievement in a continuing series of efforts to reconcile value and concrete reality in the contemporary theatre.

To solve the problem of dramatic vocality, Eliot resorted to the Christian concept of sacramental time, the formulation of which goes back to patristic Biblical exegesis. His preoccupation with the theme of time, particularly in the *Four Quartets,* has, of course, often been noted. What needs pointing out, however, is that the view of time he holds is implicitly an aesthetic principle,[5] one which has important implications for the modern artist and particularly for the poetic dramatist who is seeking to break through the surface of naturalistic drama to achieve a multivocal action without sacrificing concreteness and particularity, a sense of the real world.

Grounded in the doctrine of the Incarnation, which in a moment of history reunites fallen man and nature with eternity, the sacramental view sees time as an eternal present, and history in general, the pattern of human events, as a "kind of incarnation or true analogue" of the eternal design of God.[6] Thus it interprets the particular human event typologically or, to be more precise, in terms of the *figura,* the analysis of which we owe to the great German philologist, Erich Auerbach. In a *figura* two persons or events of different times, the sacrifice of Isaac and the sacrifice of Christ, for example, are related in such a way that the first signifies not only itself but also the second, while the second encloses or fulfills the first; yet both point to a third, no less real, image in the future which will be the ultimate fulfillment of the first two events. Neither of the two events in time, then, has the factual self-sufficiency, the sense of finality, that the naturalistic or scientific interpretation of time accords to events. Nor, on the other hand, are they merely abstract, ahistorical mirrors or copies of a complete Idea as a neo-Platonic interpretation of time would have it. Both remain real but incomplete, subordinated to the real future event which will fulfill them. Accord-

---

[3] *The Plays of T. S. Eliot* (London, 1960), p. 81.

[4] *The Third Voice* (Princeton, 1959), p. 75.

[5] The only two critics, as far as I know, who have perceived the aesthetic implications of Eliot's sacramental vision are Malcolm Mackenzie Ross, *Poetry and Dogma* (New Brunswick, New Jersey, 1954) and Charles Moorman, *Arthurian Triptych* (Berkeley, 1960). Neither, however, applies his insight to Eliot's verse drama, where, it seems to me, the sacramental aesthetic is more relevant to the art form. Ross's reference to Eliot's sacramentalism is incidental, and Moorman's is limited to a discussion of *The Waste Land.*

[6] Ross, p. 88.

ingly, they are integrally, i.e., analogically, related, not horizontally in the temporal dimension, but by their vertical relationship to the eternal design that has always existed, yet is to be fulfilled in the historical future.[7]

In *Murder in the Cathedral*, Eliot employs the term "figure" on two crucial occasions to characterize the action he is dramatizing. This is no mere synonym for "metaphor". For his interpretation of the murder of Thomas Becket corresponds closely to the medieval definition of the *figura*. Thomas and, through Thomas, the Women of Canterbury are shown coming to perceive the Incarnation of Christ not only as a moment in the historical past but also as a moment that extends through time, as an eternally present act, and, accordingly, the action in which they are participating not as an inconsequential accident in English history, but as a significant event simultaneously in and beyond history. Eliot thus interprets the murder as a *figura Christi*, a sacramental action, itself and other than itself, that confirms or fulfills in a moment of time the redemptive function of the real and archetypal sacrifice of Christ and that prefigures at the same time the final fulfillment of the eternal pattern.

The *figura*, then, though it is essentially a Christian method of historical interpretation, is also an aesthetic principle. The figural imitation of a historical event such as the murder of Becket results in a dramatic action which transcends without negating its historical pastness: through the event's analogical relationships with a previous event (in the case of Becket, the sacrifice of Christ) and with the eternal pattern which is figured in both, the image of the historical action assumes a symbolic significance for all time. Figural imitation, then, is a genuinely poetic mode of representing reality. It renders actions at once concrete and significant, particular and universal, and thus rescues value, including the value of the past, from naturalism and concrete reality from "angelism."

In order to give his historical action a symbolic dimension and accordingly contemporary relevance without sacrificing its historicity, then, Eliot resorts to the strategy of figural imitation. He projects Thomas's murder, the present action, as an analogy of the archetypal *figura*, the Sacrifice, or rather the Incarnation, of Christ, which prefigures the action, clarifies its significance, and extends its effect beyond itself. Though Thomas's Christmas morning sermon contains a direct definition of the analogy, Eliot's primary means of achieving the figural

[7] "Figura," *Scenes from the Drama of European Literature* (New York, 1959), p. 59. See also *Mimesis* (Garden City, 1957), pp. 64–66 and 136–41.

relationship between past and present, Christ and Thomas, is both subtler and more organic. He shapes the action of Thomas's murder within a matrix of various kinds of verbal and visual references and allusions which evoke the pattern of the Incarnation: the Coming, the Temptation, the Passion and the Redemption.

The first phase of the Christic pattern is established by references to "the Coming", which reverberate like musical phrases throughout Part I. Though these references are literally to the coming of Thomas to Canterbury after his seven years of exile (the reiteration of this sacred number gives it a symbolic dimension; it becomes a part of the "coming" complex, signifying the end and the beginning), the simultaneous association with the coming of the new year and the coming of Christ is insistent, thus suggesting the end of a figural cycle and the beginning of another, which in turn suggests the eternal presentness of the Incarnation. At the beginning of the action, the Women intuitively recognize Thomas's return from France to be one with the coming of the terrible spring and of Christ:

> The New Year waits, destiny waits for the coming . . .
> [Who has] Remembered the martyrs and saints who
> wait? and who shall
> Stretch out his hand to the fire, and deny his
> master? [8]

> Winter shall come bringing death from the sea,
> Ruinous spring shall beat at our doors. . . .
> Some malady is coming upon us. We wait, we wait,
> And the saints and martyrs wait, for those who
> shall be martyrs and saints. (p. 176)
> Come, happy December, who shall observe you,
> who shall preserve you?
> Shall the Son of Man be born again in the litter
> of scorn? (p. 177)

The references are then picked up by the Priests of Canterbury, but now they are in ironic counterpoint to the dignity the prophetic Women give them. The First Priest, echoing the Women, begins the movement: "Seven years and the summer is over. / Seven years since the Archbishop left us" (p. 177). Shortly after, a Herald enters to give them

[8] T. S. Eliot, *Murder in the Cathedral*, in *The Complete Poems and Plays, 1909–1950* (New York, 1952), pp. 175–76. Further citations will be incorporated in parentheses in the text. The analogy between Thomas and Christ is enforced by the reference to Peter's denial of "his master."

"notice of his coming" (p. 177), and to describe Thomas's reception in terms evoking Christ's entry into Jerusalem:

> He comes in pride and sorrow, affirming all his claims,
> Assured, beyond doubt, of the devotion of the people,
> Who receive him with scenes of frenzied enthusiasm,
> Lining the road and throwing down their capes,
> Strewing the way with leaves and late flowers of the season.[9]

The recital reaches its climax with the Second Priest's attempt to allay the worldly fears of his colleagues: "Yet our lord is returned. Our lord has come back to his own again" (p. 179). In his summarizing speech, the Third Priest gathers the references to the coming into a partial expression of the central symbol of the Incarnation—the still and turning wheel—thus preparing for its full revelation:

> For good or ill, let the wheel turn.
> The wheel has been still, these seven years, and
>   no good.
> For ill or good, let the wheel turn.   (p. 179)

In the final movement of this section, the Women, with Thomas's arrival imminent, return to the theme of the coming. They identify it now with the coming of a cosmic death—"You come with applause, you come with rejoicing, but you come bringing death into Canterbury" (p. 180)—and by incantatory repetition of the reverse of the image seek to prevent the coming:

> O Thomas, return, Archbishop; return, return to France . . .
> O Thomas, Archbishop, leave us, leave us, leave
>   sullen Dover, and set sail for France.   (pp. 180–1)

With Thomas's arrival, the references to the coming are finally resolved in the wheel symbol. Rebuking the Second Priest for chiding the Women, Thomas reveals that "they know and do not know" that the coming they fear is the coming of the still point, a figure of the Incarnation, into the round of their lives. But since Thomas also knows and does not know, the end of this movement is a new beginning, which, through the second phase of the Christic action, the Temptation, will lead to a full understanding of the sacramental import of his coming.

Thus, without sacrificing dramatic effects such as irony and the ten-

---

[9] P. 178. Cf. Matthew 21:8–9: "Most of the crowd spread their garments on the road, and others cut branches from trees and spread them on the road. And the crowds that went before him and that followed him shouted 'Hosanna to the Son of David! Blessed is he who comes in the name of the Lord!' "

sion of unresolved action, Eliot not only succeeds in establishing the image of Christ, the first pole of the *figura,* in the historical action, but also goes far in revealing the sacramental significance of the Incarnation on which the meaning and form of the drama rest.

Eliot establishes the second and third phases of the *figura Christi* by representing the temptation and conversion of Thomas as analogous to Christ's temptation in the desert and His commitment to finitude, that is, by representing the four tempters in terms of time and eternity and Thomas's peripety in terms of the Incarnation, which reconciles the antinomies.

The conventional interpretation of the first three tempters places them on the plane of worldly satisfactions, the first representing sensual pleasures, and the second and third, political power. This reading lacks focus. It fixes the action on a level that, in terms of the play as a whole, is peripheral and therefore distorts its real meaning. Examined in their dramatic contexts, the speeches of the three tempters are seen to orient Thomas's vision in the directions of the past, the present, and the future, that is, on the plane of time. Seen in this light, the first three tempters prepare us to interpret the Fourth as an embodiment not only of Becket's pride but also, and more accurately, of his "angelic" vision —his desire to circumvent the time world in the pursuit of essence— and therefore to discover the sacramental nature of his conversion.

The First Tempter advocates not merely the life of pleasure, but a return to the "good time past," to self-indulgent youth. That it is the temporal orientation, the past, which is important in the temptation is revealed by the whole tenor of Thomas's reaction: "You talk of seasons that are past. I remember / Not worth forgetting." [10] The Second Tempter urges Thomas not merely to seize temporal power, but to seize it now, in the present moment, while the king is away. He warns him against two kinds of "deceitful shadows," against "mirth merry-making" and "godlovers' longing," the past and timelessness, and insists repeatedly, "Power is present. Holiness hereafter" (p. 186). Finally, the Third Tempter counsels Thomas not merely to ally himself with the barons against the king in a struggle for power, but to join "in the fight for liberty," to live, in other words, for the future: "time past is time forgotten. / We expect the rise of a new constellation" (p. 189). That the "new constellation" implies to Thomas democracy and therefore emphasizes future possibilities is clearly revealed in his climactic rejection: "It is not better to be thrown / To a thousand hungry appe-

---

[10] P. 184. See also p. 185, where Thomas's concluding contrast of the dead past with the present leads directly into the second temptation, which is oriented in the present.

tites than to one. / At a future time this may be shown" (p. 189). The first three tempters, then, represent above all historical time or the world in its three temporal manifestations. Ultimately, they represent a mode of perception that gives the human will the authority, limited only by its mortality, to control events, and makes man the measure of all temporal things.

Becket's repudiation of the first three tempters is motivated by his awareness of his election to martyrdom. This is ostensibly grounded in a mode of perception which is the opposite of the tempters' naturalistic vision, one, he thinks, which is in accord with the will of God. Actually, however, his agons with the three tempters reveal his unwillingness to descend to earthly considerations (the imagery representing Thomas as an eagle soaring high above the lower orders is pervasive), an over-weening pride based on an angelic, not a temporal, point of view. There is, then, something radically wrong with his vision.

In the initial encounter, the First Tempter asserts, "Your Lordship is too proud!" (p. 184), and following the Archbishop's curt and final dismissal, concludes enigmatically, "Then I leave you to your fate. / I leave you to the pleasures of your higher vices, / Which will have to be paid for at higher prices" (p. 184). In the second encounter the reference to Thomas's angelism is even more emphatic. Against the tempter's advocacy of present power, Thomas opposes "Holiness":

> shall I, who keep the keys
> Of heaven and hell, supreme alone in England,
> Who bind and loose, with power from the Pope,
> Descend to desire a punier power?   (p. 187)

But it is obviously a tainted holiness, which the Second Tempter, like the First, recognizes when he too concludes: "Then I leave you to your fate. / Your sin soars sunward, covering kings' falcons" (p. 187). In the third encounter, Becket's angelic perspective is less explicit though no less present: "Shall I who ruled like an eagle over doves / Now take the shape of a wolf among wolves?" (p. 189).

Thus when Thomas has dismissed his "temporal tempters" (p. 193) and is confronted by the Fourth Tempter, it is with surprise and reluctance that he receives the unexpected visitor. But the Tempter is aware that the Archbishop has prepared for him:

> As you do not know me, I do not need a name,
> And, as you know me, that is why I come.
> You know me but have never seen my face.
> To meet before was never time or place.
>
> (p. 190)

The Fourth Tempter's explanation in the last line implies his nature. Appearing only when Thomas's rejection of time is complete, he represents a spiritual rather than a secular attitude. He advocates perception from the vantage point of the fourth dimension of time, eternity, and thus is the embodiment of the vision Thomas opposes to the temporal point of view of the first three tempters. This is clearly indicated by his ironic repetition of the metaphor of the keys of heaven and hell that Thomas has used against the Second Tempter:

> Fare forward to the end.
> All other ways are closed to you
> Except the way already chosen. . . .
> You hold the keys of heaven and hell.
> Power to bind and loose: bind, Thomas, bind,
> King and bishop under your heel. . . .
> To be master or servant within an hour,
> This is the course of temporal power. . . .
> You hold the skein: wind, Thomas, wind
> The thread of eternal life and death.
>
> (p. 191)

In other words, Becket's last temptation represents the egocentric Satanic vision: the desire to perceive as God, to be outside of time, thus avoiding the limitations of mortality, yet to control it, to keep it on its knees perpetually:

> Saint and Martyr rule from the tomb.
> Think, Thomas, think of enemies dismayed,
> Creeping in penance, frightened of a shade;
> Think of pilgrims, standing in line
> Before the glittering jewelled shrine,
> From generation to generation
> Bending the knee in supplication.
>
> (pp. 191–2)

And that, of course, is why the fourth temptation is "the greatest treason" (p. 196).

What, then, is the authentic vision, the alternative to the naturalism of the first three tempters, if angelic perception leads to "the right deed for the wrong reason?" Taking advantage of Becket's agonized recognition and acknowledgement of his "soul's sickness" (p. 193), the Fourth Tempter, is one of the great ironies of the play, repeats the words the archbishop had spoken, without complete awareness of their meaning we now realize, to the Women of Canterbury at the beginning of the action:

> You know and do not know, what it is to act or suffer.
> You know and do not know, that acting is suffering,
> And suffering action. Neither does the actor suffer
> Nor the patient act. But both are fixed
> In an eternal action, an eternal patience
> To which all must consent that it may be willed
> And which all must suffer that they may will it,
> That the pattern may subsist, that the wheel may
>   turn and still
> Be forever still.   (p. 193)

Until this point in the action, Thomas has seen Being as a wheel of which the center and circumference, that is, eternity and time, God and the creation, are dissociated and opposite entities, the center, as active agent, arbitrarily moving the circumference. Accordingly, Thomas has unwittingly but actively sought to escape from the circumference into the center, from which point he can control the movement of the circumference. This interpretation of the action is enforced by two references to the wheel which pertain directly to Thomas's mode of perception. The first occurs in his encounter with the First Tempter. To the latter's suggestion that he make the winter of his age a spring, Thomas replies: "Only / The fool fixed in his folly, may think / He can turn the wheel on which he turns" (p. 184). Here Thomas sees himself on the circumference, but the discontinuity of eternity and time is implied dramatically in the disdain he reveals for the life in time. The second reference occurs significantly in his encounter with the Fourth Tempter. This time it is the tempter who employs the image:

> You have also thought, sometimes at your prayers, . . .
> That nothing lasts, but the wheel turns, . . .
> That the shrine shall be pillaged, and the gold spent. . . .
> When miracles cease, and the faithful desert you,
> And men shall only do their best to forget you.
> And later is worse, when men will not hate you
> Enough to defame or to execrate you,
> But pondering the qualities that you lacked
> Will only try to find the historical fact.   (p. 192)

What was ambiguous in Thomas's reference to the wheel is made explicit in the Fourth Tempter's projection of Thomas's thoughts.

Martyrdom for him is at once a means of escape from the circumference, where, according to his discontinuous view of Being, "nothing lasts," and of achieving the center, from which he can move the circumference.

What Thomas realizes when the Fourth Tempter reverts to his earlier speech is that the center and circumference are not discontinuous. He sees rather that the center represents a reconciliation of eternity and time, God and the creation, action and suffering, and that this pattern is figured, however grossly, on the circumference. The role, therefore, of those in the perpetually changing world of time is not to escape it, but to achieve within and in behalf of time an analogous reconciliation of action (the will *seeking* the permanence of eternity) and suffering (the will *consenting* to the operation of eternity), a patient activeness (the martyr) or an active patience (the community), "That the pattern may subsist, that the wheel may turn and still / Be forever still."

In apprehending the eternal design in the flux of time, Thomas bears witness to the Incarnation, which Eliot defines in "The Dry Salvages" as "The point of intersection of the timeless / With time," where "the past and future / Are conquered and reconciled." [11] He bears witness, that is, to the act of love that redeems and thus infuses time with sacramental significance. He accepts—and his acceptance becomes a figure of—what William Lynch, in a discussion of the Temptation in the desert, calls "the great qualitative leap into the human way . . . found in the New Law with Christ the second Adam as its athlete in the confrontation of the finite." [12] Accordingly, he now perceives his martyrdom as an integral part of God's design initiated by the Incarnation, and he submits his will to it. On the analogy of Christ's decisive assumption of flesh, he descends in Love into time and thus achieves the reconciliation of action and suffering that brings him the peace he defines in his sermon, the "still point" in his own life, and prepares him for true martyrdom. This is conclusively established in his last words in Part I: "I shall no longer act or suffer, to the sword's end" (p. 197). In the words of his Christmas morning sermon, which expresses his achieved epiphany, his recognition of the integral relationship between sacramental vision and the Incarnation, he becomes the

---

[11] "Four Quartets," *The Complete Poems and Plays*, p. 136.

[12] "Theology and the Imagination: I," *Thought*, XXIX, 112 (March, 1954), 72. Lynch continues in the same passage: "His [Christ's assumption of finitude] is complete and absolute . . . . And this decision, this assumption of the path through the body, is made absolute and irrevocable in the scene of the desert temptation where Christ tempted to the way of magic and tricks and *the direct use of glory and the infinite* chooses the human way." My italics.

paradoxical free "instrument of God" (p. 199) in time, and his martyrdom "a smaller figure" (p. 199) of the sacrifice of Christ that extends
the Redemption through time.[13]

Becket's sermon, as Louis Martz points out, is a nodus that binds the
two parts of the action together.[14] In it, Thomas explains that the
martyr is made not only for the glory of God, but also for the salvation
of men. For the martyrdom to be efficacious, the community must, like
the martyr, undergo a process of enlightenment. The sermon not only
defines the figural relation between Thomas and Christ, but also,
though implicitly, that between the Women of Canterbury and the
Christian community contemporary with Christ in their roles as witnesses of the sacrifice, as sharers "of the eternal burden" (p. 208). It is
the second analogy that receives primary emphasis in Part II of *Murder
in the Cathedral*.

In "The Dry Salvages," Eliot says that "to apprehend the point of
intersection of the timeless / With time, is an occupation for the
Saint. . . ." For the mass of mankind there are only "hints and
guesses." [15] Thus, whereas the divinely elected Thomas is an active
witness, the earthbound Chorus is essentially a passive witness. But just
as Thomas must "descend," bringing the eternal design into time, and
submit to a passive activeness in fulfillment of his purpose, the Women
must "ascend," bringing time into the eternal design, and *consent* to
an active patience. They must willingly lay themselves open to the
operation of Providence.

In Part I of the play, we see the Chorus immersed in the flux of naturalistic time. They have a dark foreboding of the cataclysmic action
that is about to break into and reverberate through the world they
inhabit. Although they unconsciously identify the coming of Thomas
with the Coming of Christ and the seasonal cycle, they are nevertheless
reluctant to acknowledge this figure of the Incarnation and the part
they must play in its realization. They desire to avoid contact with the
center that turns the circumference, fearing the communal engagement

---

[13] Denis Donoghue's comment about the tempters is characteristic of the criticism
that fails to perceive the four tempters on the level of time: "The nature of the
Archbishop's character and of his past life is filled out by [the temptations]; his
present spiritual condition is clarified, both to himself and to his audience, by the
Fourth Tempter. These, then, are the functions of agents whose presence in the play
seems at first sight a rather trite association of Thomas with the tempted Christ."
The Third Voice, p. 86. Seen on the level of time these encounters *establish* the
figural dimension of the play.

[14] "The Wheel and the Point," *T. S. Eliot, A Selected Critique,* ed. Leonard Unger
(New York, 1948), p. 461.

[15] "Four Quartets," p. 136.

demanded by the life in sacramental time. They prefer the "quiet seasons" (p. 176) and seek "to pass unobserved" (p. 176), to preserve their inert existence, its irresponsible privacy, and its inconsequential regularity:

> We do not wish anything to happen.
> Seven years we have lived quietly,
> Succeeded in avoiding notice,
> Living and partly living . . . .
> We have kept the feasts, heard the masses,
> We have brewed beer and cyder,
> Gathered wood against the winter, . . .
> We have seen births, deaths and marriages, . . .
> We have all had our private terrors,
> Our particular shadows, our secret fears.
> But now a great fear is upon us, a fear not of
>   one but of many,
> A fear like birth and death, when we see birth and
>   death alone
> In a void apart.   (pp. 180–1)

Although the Women recognize their passive role on the circumference of Being—"For us the poor, there is no action / But only to wait and to witness" (p. 177)—their passivity is that of the semiconscious animal. Thus in order to truly bear witness, to activate their passivity, they must come to perceive communally the eternal design operating in time.

The first decisive step in the agonizing process towards bearing their "share of the eternal burden" is taken when the Women witness Thomas's first encounter with the four knights and realize the inevitability of his murder. They perceive the evil in the world in a vision of a chaotic universe, where the orders of time and of creatures are abolished,[16] become conscious of their involvement in the universal disorder, and paradoxically recognize that what they had persuaded themselves were merely the natural and inconsequential accidents of otherwise orderly lives in time are actually manifestations of the pattern of radical sin inherent in created things. The impending murder of Thomas, they admit, "was here, in the kitchen, in the passage, / In the mews in the barn in the byre in the market place / In our veins our bowels our skulls as well / As well as in the plottings of potentates. . . ." (p. 208), thus acknowledging their collective guilt.

---

[16] Martz, p. 458.

In their next utterance, shortly before the murder, the Women perceive with horror that the ultimate result of their sin is total separation
from God, entry into the Void "Where the soul is no longer deceived,
for there are no objects, no tones, / No colours, no forms to distract, to
divert the soul / From seeing itself, foully united forever, nothing with
nothing" (p. 210), and in their hour of need they are driven to call out
for an intercessor. Their acceptance of responsibility for the imminent
death of Thomas, of their "[consent] to the last humiliation" (p. 208),
has become the positive or active consent to the operation of the eternal
design in their lives.

With the murder of Thomas, the terrible action is consummated; it
has come full circle. The Women of Canterbury can no longer "pass
unobserved" on the circumference of the wheel of Being: "How can I
ever return to the soft quiet seasons?" (p. 214). Here for the last time
the Women revert to the three-stress line which catalogues life on the
circumference, but now it is presented in the past tense to reveal the
end of the cycle: "We did not wish anything to happen. / We understood the private catastrophe. . . . / Living and partly living . . ."
(p. 214). Through the murder, they too, in their own way, have borne
witness to the awful reality of the eternal pattern. They have been
shaken into a collective consciousness of their integral relation to the
still point, the center of the wheel. Their witness, it is true, is a negative
one. All their diffuse intimations of evil operating in time have coa-
lesced in the moment of martyrdom into a vision of a pattern which
is the absolute opposite of the Incarnation: "An *instant eternity* of evil
and wrong." [17] But the recognition of the one, which is the Fall, leads
simultaneously to the awareness and acceptance of the other, which is
the Redemption. "The darkness," the Women affirm at the end, "declares the glory of light" (p. 220). Thus in their final chorus, they
express their new, their sacramental vision of the universe. Now,
through the sacrifice of Christ renewed in the martyrdom of Thomas,
through the ultimate reconciliation of time and eternity, all the irre-
concilables of life in naturalistic time—nature and spirit, man and
beast, the pattern of man's life and the pattern of the seasons, and past,
present, and future—are reconciled and reintegrated into a grand
sacramental image of the eternal design. This new vision completes
what Thomas has called "the figure of God's purpose" (p. 208).

Figural or sacramental interpretation is not restricted to establishing
analogical relationships between events in the Christian era. Although,
as Auerbach shows, the method arose out of the need of the Christian

[17] P. 214. My italics.

Fathers to bring the events of the Old Testament into harmony with those described in the New Testament without negating their historicity, it was not long before other historical lacunae in the Christian narrative, pagan and profane, came to be interpreted in the light of the New Testament:[18] the universal Roman monarchy, for example, became for Dante a *figura* of the Kingdom of God.[19] The point is that the seed of wider application is inherent in the method. The ultimate function of figural interpretation is, as Malcolm Ross notes, to integrate *all* history, including *all* human knowledge early and late, into the universal design of Christianity.[20]

Whether or not such a synthesis is possible in our time is outside the bounds of this discussion, but that the figural method is salutary for art, and particularly for drama, is clearly indicated in *Murder in the Cathedral* by the figural use to which Eliot puts not only specifically Christian events but also modern anthropological knowledge. Thus besides the figure of Christ, he integrates a second figural level, pre-Christian, though drawn from the realm of modern anthropological knowledge: the dying corn God of the pagan fertility religions, whose sacrificial death renews the land and the community.

The figural relationship between the Waste Land-dying god complex and the Women of Canterbury-Thomas-Christ complex is, we recall, established in the first chorus and sustained and developed throughout the action. It reaches a climax in the chorus following the murder, when the Women, overwhelmed by their corporate guilt, see the blood of the hero as the ultimate defilement of nature: "The land is foul, the water is foul, our beasts and ourselves defiled with blood" (p. 214). It culminates in the final chorus, when the Women, having perceived that the blood of Thomas "forever renews the earth" (p. 221), express their vision, already referred to, of the fructification of their lives and the life of nature.[21]

The parallel in the play between the seasonal death and renewal and Christian martyrdom has, of course, often been noted. What has not, however—and it is a crucial omission in the criticism of *Murder in the Cathedral* and of Eliot's plays in general—is the operative aesthetic principle that unites the three levels organically, that, in the phrase Eliot uses in reference to the Metaphysical poets, "is constantly amalga-

---

[18] Auerbach, "Figura," pp. 63–64 and *Mimesis,* p. 13.

[19] *Mimesis,* p. 170ff.

[20] *Poetry and Dogma,* p. 247. Actually Professor Ross employs the term "sacramentalism" rather than "figural interpretation" but the two are broadly synonymous.

[21] The renewal, of course, is not merely a matter of fertility. It is also, as Jones notes, "a matter of securing the divinely ordained order of Nature" (p. 75).

mating disparate experience:" [22] the principle of figural or sacramental interpretation which is grounded in the Incarnation, where the "impossible union / Of spheres of existence is actual." [23] Failure to perceive this principle results in an embarrassing inability to account for the integral relation of the various levels of reference that permeate the play. Even as perceptive a commentator on the play as Miss Patricia Adair obscures rather than clarifies the art of *Murder in the Cathedral* when she writes:

> To express [the theme of life coming through death] Mr. Eliot sometimes uses the Christian symbolism of the Cross, blood, redemption; but his more frequently used and far more powerful image is much older than Christianity. It is the image of the Seasons, the death and renewal of the earth, which has been woven into the rhythms of man's life from primeval times.[24]

This criticism lacks focus. The implied qualitative distinction between the Christian symbolism and the seasonal imagery suggests that the relationship between the two is mechanical, that the levels are "yoked by violence together." Recognition of the figural principle clearly reveals them to be "amalgamated," a single image.

Through the figural aesthetic Eliot creates an experience that is valid both within and beyond the bounds of the conventional conception of the Christian era. What is necessary for the understanding and appreciation of the play, even though it is about Christian martyrdom and its deepest level of meaning lies in this theme, is not so much formal belief in Christianity as sacramental vision, which is an aesthetic as well as a theological principle.

But, of course, Eliot cannot count on an audience, even a Christian audience, whose imagination is oriented sacramentally. The aesthetic sensibility he must address is that which perceives according to the dictates of the modern naturalistic view of time, that interprets past events as irrevocably past and finds them interesting only for their sensational violence, or, at best, their rational-historical cause. Eliot's dramatic problem is therefore double: not only has he to create a viable dramatic action but also and simultaneously a dramatic form capable of animating, at least for the period of the play, the dormant sacramental imagination of his audience. He has to dissolve its naturalistic time-consciousness so that it may perceive the action not as a mur-

---

[22] Eliot, "The Metaphysical Poets," *Selected Essays* (New York, 1950), p. 247.
[23] "Four Quartets," p. 136.
[24] Patricia Adair, "Mr. Eliot's *Murder in the Cathedral*," *Cambridge Journal*, IV, 2 (November, 1950), p. 89.

der or a suicide or an interesting case history, but as a martyrdom, or sacrifice, that has communal and lasting significance.

Here again the figural aesthetic provides Eliot with a solution. Since the *figura* not only relates past events and absorbs them into the universal design but also and primarily looks to the future, to the ultimate concrete fulfillment, it tends to impose on the dramatic form conventions that relate the figural action and the contemporary audience. Thus the formal framework that Eliot adopts to contain the action is, as Ronald Peacock points out, broadly liturgical, consisting of a series of "direct links at various points with [the] audience"—the choruses, portions of Becket's speeches preceding and following the temptations, the sermon, the four Knights' defense. But the function of these is not only to make the work "a continuous invitation to celebrate in religious fellowship the spiritual triumph of a saint," as Peacock notes.[25] They also serve to reorient the time-mind of the twentieth-century audience and to focus it on the figural nature of Thomas's murder without resorting to the "harangue" that mars Eliot's *The Rock* and other earlier Christian drama.[26] As in the thematic development, the distinction which these links exploit is, on the level of perception, that between naturalistic and sacramental time, and, on the corollary level of moral significance, that between murder or suicide (the moral import of the act seen from the point of view of naturalistic time) and martyrdom (its moral import seen from the point of view of sacramental time). At first, the audience is identified with the naturalistic time mind. As the action develops, however, and the audience begins to realize its sacramental significance, the links, both directly and indirectly, give impetus to the reorientation.

The function of the Chorus in this respect has already been suggested. As "the type of the common man" (p. 221) it mediates between the audience and the action, its development guiding that of the audience, which it represents. It is therefore the least direct link. More overt and perhaps bolder, though no less justified by the figural method, are the other links involving direct appeal to the audience.

After he has apprehended the sacramental significance of his election to martyrdom, Thomas turns to the modern audience, which is by now uneasy about the "historical" event, the "murder in the cathedral" it is witnessing, and identifies its superficial, its prosaic, historical consciousness:

> What yet remains to show you of my history
> Will seem to most of you at best futility,

[25] *The Poet in the Theater* (New York, 1946), p. 7.
[26] Eliot, "The Three Voices of Poetry," *On Poetry and Poets* (London, 1942), p. 91.

Senseless self-slaughter of a lunatic,
Arrogant passion of a fanatic.
I know that history at all times draws
The strangest consequence from remotest cause.

(p. 197)

This serves to shock the audience out of its habitual refuge in naturalistic time. In the sermon which follows, Thomas again addresses the
audience. Here he not only distinguishes between naturalistic perception and sacramental vision—("as the World sees, this [the simultaneous celebration of the Birth and Death of Christ] is to behave in a
strange fashion.") (p. 198)—but also, as we have seen, clarifies the nature of sacramental vision and thus prepares the audience to apprehend
the murder sacramentally.

After the murder, when the Four Knights step forward to defend
their act before the audience, it is from the point of view of the modern
conception of time, the point of view that Thomas had attributed earlier to the audience, that the defense is carried out. They assume the
cause-effect approach of the court room or of the naturalistic drama
(along with its "commonsense," prose idiom), and present the murder
of Thomas as "a problem," "a case," which one of the knights entitles,
after Agatha Christie, "Who Killed the Archbishop?" They identify
their "reasonable" secular motives with the desires of the audience—
"We have served your interests. . . ." (p. 218)—and after summing up
"the facts" of Becket's irrational behavior, ask the audience, in words
which echo the Archbishop's direct address, that they "unhesitatingly
render a verdict of Suicide while of Unsound Mind" (p. 219). But now
the audience cannot but see the shallowness of, and be repelled by, the
Knights' (which has been their own) reasonable point of view. Through
the formal conventions inhering in the figural method—the links that
make the audience participants in the action—Eliot, then, not only
clarifies the distinctions that terminate in a single action, but also traps
(in Denis de Rougemont's sense of the word)[27] his audience into perceiving it sacramentally without recourse to palpable design.[28]

---

[27] Denis de Rougemont, "Religion and The Mission of the Artist" in *Spiritual Problems in Contemporary Literature*, ed. by Stanley R. Hopper (New York, 1957). "I
define it [the nature of the work of art] as a *calculated trap* for meditation, we see
that the understanding of its nature is tied up with that of its end: a trap is made in
order to capture something. In the work of art, nature and aim, essence and end, are
inseparable. It is a question of a single and identical function, which is, to signify
something by sensible means." (p. 177.)

[28] Hugh Kenner sees the dramatic problem similarly, but describes Eliot's solution
in the light of the "contrast lurking in every detective story, the contrast between

In *Murder in the Cathedral*, then, T. S. Eliot, by means of the figural aesthetic, transcends the univocal realism of naturalistic drama without resorting to the strategy that altogether by-passes or dissolves concrete reality and thus destroys the essential form of drama and negates its public function. It is true that Eliot fails to "naturalize" the action to the extent demanded by the figural aesthetic, which suggests that his respect for history and human events is at this point a grudging one. But the commonly held pejorative conclusion that the play is an allegory, "a demonstration of a particular theological idea," as Francis Fergusson puts it,[29] is an unsatisfactory one. For *Murder in the Cathedral* is more "naturalistic" than most critics are willing to admit. This can be seen not only in the unconscious pride, noted above, that Thomas reveals throughout Part I, but also, as D. E. S. Maxwell shows, in the ironic humor he manifests in his encounters with the first three tempters and especially in the considerable internal conflict mirrored in his confrontation with the Fourth Tempter.[30] But it is in Part II that the primary evidence lies. Here Eliot patently represents the murder of Thomas in the naturalistic mode. This has been remarked by some critics, but it is usually judged as a serious flaw in the allegorical structure.[31] When, however, the naturalism of Part II is seen in the light of Thomas's achievement at the end of Part I of sacramental vision and his consequent descent into time, the humanity of Thomas becomes an integral part of an action that is conceived and at least partially executed by Eliot not as an illustration of a theological principle but as a sacramental image or symbol that is at once itself and other than itself, historical and eternal, transitory and permanent, real and significant.

The recognition of the figural or sacramental aesthetic as the operative principle of *Murder in the Cathedral* is a necessary condition of

---

actions as they are performed . . . and the same actions as the Sleuth glibly recounts them in his context of omniscience." Thus "Eliot's ingenious stratagem was to give the first telling the substantiality of dramatic exhibition and produce the glib summing up as a fatuous anticlimax." *The Invisible Poet: T. S. Eliot* (New York, 1959), p. 282. What Kenner fails to reveal, however, is that this final ironic distinction is made possible by Eliot's imaginative use of the links inhering on the figural method.

[29] *The Idea of a Theater* (Princeton, 1949), p. 229.

[30] *The Poetry of T. S. Eliot* (London, 1952), p. 183.

[31] Kenner's comment on this is typical: "The first [of those things that tend to obscure the changed orientation of Becket's will] is the effectiveness of the second act, which so impresses us with Becket's human force, his energetic fortitude before death, that the interchange with the Fourth Tempter is obliterated from memory, and thus rendered inaccessible to the Fourth Knight's suicide verdict which ought to have recalled it and brought it viably into salience at the climax of the play." *The Invisible Poet*, p. 283.

perceiving the continuity of Eliot's efforts in the poetic drama. For it is the figural aesthetic that governs the formal characteristics of the action and of the language, the verse, of *all* Eliot's plays. It is the means by which he integrates Greek and Christian myth into the action and achieves the ironic distinctions between the action seen naturalistically and sacramentally in his later plays. (In *The Family Reunion,* to mention the most obvious example, the distinction between crime-punishment and sin-expiation is analogous to the distinction between murder and martyrdom in *Murder in the Cathedral.*) Finally, since the figural aesthetic exacts respect for concrete reality and points insistently to the future, it lies behind Eliot's acknowledgement of the claims of the present, the contemporary scene, and his progressive efforts to achieve a more "naturalistic" action and verse. It is the failure to recognize the figural aesthetic in *Murder in the Cathedral* that has led critics to conclude that the play is a throwback to nineteenth-century drama, or at best a *tour de force* but a dead end. Its recognition, on the contrary, reveals that the play is a crucial experiment in Eliot's efforts to revitalize the modern poetic drama and a point of departure for his later achievements in this genre.

PART TWO

Spokes of the Wheel

IN THE CATHEDRAL

Patricia M. Adair

If we forget that Mr. T. S. Eliot's *Murder in the Cathedral* was written for production at Canterbury, we fail to understand the play. Much of its true significance is lost on the stage. For the theatre is, above all, rich with humanity, vibrating to the suffering and laughter and ecstasy of human beings. Across the footlights the quiver of human emotion passes back and forth from actors to audience, as men and women share the fuller, intenser, more amusing life of the characters who strut and fret, magnified and vivid before them. But what significance has the human figure in the vast, echoing cathedral of Canterbury? At the foot of those tremendous pillars no man is of any stature, no human voice can reach that spreading roof. Every mounting curve and stone proclaim that this is a church, designed for the worship of God, where the tombs of the famous dead and the footsteps of the living are equally unimportant. Is it possible, then, to judge a play written with this setting in mind by ordinary dramatic standards? *Murder in the Cathedral* is a religious drama, the story of Canterbury's most famous saint, with the emphasis laid on Becket's bitter fulfilment of God's purpose rather than on his humanity. Indeed a study of Mr. Eliot's sources suggests that he deliberately sacrificed the warmth and vitality and ironic vigour of the Thomas his contemporaries knew, in subjugation to his religious conception of sainthood and martyrdom. He is concerned above all to show us the ways of God to man or perhaps, more truly, the ways of man to God, not only in the twelfth but in the twentieth century, and to that purpose he shapes the life and death of Thomas à Becket. A cold air stirs between the grey pillars, which dwarf the human figure; and the atmosphere of the play is cold and a little rarefied too. Seldom has a work of art been wedded so

From *Patricia Adair*, Mr. Eliot's 'Murder in the Cathedral' *from* The Cambridge Journal, *IV (October 1950–September 1951), 83. Reprinted by permission of Bowes & Bowes Publishers Ltd. Headings in Part Two are supplied by the editor.*

closely to its setting. The play itself is in two parts, divided by the Sermon, just as the cathedral is built on three levels. The drama has the same clarity of design, the same close-knit, shapely structure, the same compelling inevitability which we feel, when, on entering the great West door of Canterbury, we look straight up the soaring arches of the nave, through the choir to where the candles flicker before the High Altar.

SOURCES

J. T. Boulton

The recent publication of *English Historical Documents 1042–1189* (ed. Douglas and Greenaway) makes more readily available translated selections from the contemporary narratives of the murder of Thomas à Becket.[1] These selections bring to one's notice in a quite startling way the 'limited . . . historical facts' to which Eliot refers in *Poetry and Drama* as being to hand for the writing of *Murder in the Cathedral.* They convince the present writer that Eliot knew the narratives intimately and used them extensively where they could best assist to realize his central theme: the conflict between the values and attitudes of religion and those of 'Secularism' as he defines it in *Religion and Literature*. He says there that people who hold the assumptions of Secularism 'concern themselves only with changes of a temporal, material, and external nature; they concern themselves with morals only of a collective nature.' He then quotes from an exposition of this 'faith' which had recently caught his eye; it begins: 'In our morality the one single test of any moral question is whether it impedes or destroys in any way the power of the individual to serve the State.'[2] Now these are the assumptions which underlie the arguments and apologies of the Knights:

From "The Use of Original Sources for the Development of a Theme: Eliot in Murder in the Cathedral," by J. T. Boulton. From English, *XI, 61 (Spring, 1956), 2–8. Copyright 1956 by James T. Boulton. Reprinted by permission of the author and of* English, *the Journal of the English Association, published by Oxford University Press.*

[1] That Eliot could not (presumably) have had access to these particular translations —Professor Douglas describes the majority as 'independent' (op. cit., p. 702)—is in itself interesting in view of the argument developed in this essay.

[2] Eliot: *Selected Prose* (ed. J. Hayward, Penguin, 1953), p. 43.

they are men 'who put [their] country first'; they consider the ideal state one which unites 'spiritual and temporal administration, *under the central government';* and they approve of the 'just subordination of the *pretensions* of the Church to *the welfare of the State.'* [3] These are the 'morals of a collective nature' to which Eliot refers. Becket, on the other hand, when he overcomes the temptations, is unconcerned with 'temporal, material, and external' values:

> It is not in time that my death shall be known;
> It is out of time that my decision is taken
>
> I give my life
> To the Law of God above the Law of Man.

He has become 'the instrument of God.' Consequently, he and the Knights argue from different premises—the Fourth Knight later complains that Becket 'evaded our questions'—and whereas the Knights try to confine the argument to the question of Becket's individual responsibility to the State, Becket has in mind a quite distinct allegiance. Something of the precision with which Eliot conceived his theme becomes clearer from an examination of his handling of source material.

There is no need—even if there were space—to reproduce the whole account of Becket's martyrdom: the interested reader will find it in Professor Douglas's book. Some of the evidence must, however, be given. It is clear from the outset that once Eliot decided on the limits of the dramatic action—'I wanted to concentrate on death and martyrdom' [4] —he adhered faithfully to the outline, and often to the detail, of the events described by contemporary witnesses.

The first important debt is to Herbert of Bosham's description of Becket's journey from Sandwich to Canterbury (1 Dec. 1170) which provides Eliot (in the Messenger's speech) with the controlling idea of the resemblance to Christ's entry into Jerusalem:

> 'he was welcomed by the poor of the land as a victim sent from heaven, . . . Christ's poor received him with the victor's laurels and as the Lord's anointed. So wherever the archbishop passed, a swarm of poor folk, small and great, young and old, flocked to meet him, some prostrating themselves in the way before him, others tearing off their garments and strewing them in the way, crying aloud, again and again, "Blessed is he that cometh in the name of the Lord." '

[3] My italics. Throughout, references to the play are taken from the 1947 reprint of the 3rd edition.
[4] Eliot: *Selected Prose* (edn. cit.), p. 78.

(There is, by the way, ample justification here for a Chorus of 'poor'
women.) Eliot uses the hint well: in the Messenger's speech he gives
the audience an easily recognizable parallel (as he had done four years
earlier in *Triumphal March*), at once introducing the idea of fore-
ordained sacrifice and beginning the elaborate pattern of links between
Becket and the tradition of Christian martyrdom which is such a
marked feature of the lead-up to the murder; and the inevitable colli-
sion between the two protagonists (Becket and Henry) is also kept in
view. At once, in fact, the dual significance of events is underlined:
they are significant on the level of 'character' and *sub specie aeternitatis.*

William fitz Stephen records Becket's text for his Christmas Day sermon, but the sermon as it appears in the play is Eliot's own creation.
For this, the central point in the play where the conflict in Becket's
mind is finally resolved and the theme of sacrifice finds its most complete analysis and statement, only the gist of the final paragraph is
found in the original narrative.

The most convincing proof of Eliot's reliance on secondary material
to portray the clash of individual minds—that is, to speak in the 'third
voice' of poetry—comes in the section of the play which begins with the
entry of the Knights and ends with the murder of Becket. Apart from
choric utterances nearly the whole of this section, either in the controlling ideas or the almost exact pattern of the speeches, can be traced
to the original narrative by Edward Grim. The four Knights, 'well
known to the archbishop's household,' enter; they are offered food
which they scorn, 'thirsting for blood rather than for food'; Becket
receives them but does not immediately address them; he greets them
'in a friendly manner' but they 'straightway answered his greeting with
curses and ironically prayed that God might help him.' Eliot's interpretation of this last detail shows how vivid was his understanding of the
angered reaction of Secularism to the servant who changes his allegiance. After Becket's demand that 'These things should not be spoken
in private or in the chamber, but in public,' the Priests return and foil
the first murderous attack. Immediately following this event Grim
records the speech of fitz Urse:

> 'When the king made peace with you and all disputes were settled, he
> sent you back to your own see, as you requested; but you, in contrary
> fashion, adding insult to injury, have broken the peace, and in your pride
> have wrought evil in yourself against your lord. For those, by whose
> ministry the king's son was crowned and invested with the honours of
> sovereignty, you with obstinate pride have condemned with sentence of
> suspension. You have also bound with the chain of anathema those serv-

ants of the king by whose counsel and prudence the business of the kingdom is transacted. From this it is manifest that you would take away the crown from the king's son if you had the power. But now the plots and schemes you have hatched in order to carry out your designs against your lord the king are known to all men. Say therefore whether you are prepared to come into the king's presence and make answer to these charges.'

It is not necessary at this point to analyse the parallel speeches in *Murder in the Cathedral*: the most rapid glance will show that Eliot divides the one speech between his first three Knights, reproducing the whole content and, in places, actual phrases. The same is true of Becket's reply:

'Never was it my wish, as God is my witness, to take away the crown from my lord the king's son or to diminish his power; rather would I wish him three crowns and help him to obtain the greatest realms of the earth. . . .'

> Never was it my wish
> To uncrown the King's son, or to diminish
> His honour and power. . . .
> I would wish him three crowns rather than one.

This analysis of the interchange between Becket and the Knights could be continued, and it would show conclusively that Eliot has relied for the detail, the general tone, and the order of the speeches (even though certain phrases are transposed from their original position) on the contemporary narrative. Later, when the Knights withdraw, the Priests urge Becket that 'it was not becoming for him to absent himself from vespers'; Becket lingers, 'awaiting that happy hour of consummation,' refusing to avoid 'the executioner, that the fury of the wolves, satiated with the blood of the shepherd, might spare the sheep'—comments by Grim which Eliot gives, whole or in part, to Becket when speaking of himself. The force of Becket's command to unbar the doors was possibly suggested by Grim's descriptive title for the Archbishop, 'Christ's doughty champion,' and the speech which follows has clearly influenced Eliot's writing while agreeing with his own interpretation of the event:

'It is not meet to make a fortress of the house of prayer, the Church of Christ, which, even if it be not closed, affords sufficient protection to its children; by suffering rather than by fighting shall we triumph over the enemy; for we are come to suffer, not to resist.'

'By suffering rather than by fighting shall we triumph' is Eliot's—and

Christianity's—answer to Secularism. Had we not already had *The Waste Land* with its 'Give, Surrender, Self-Control' (although the immediate source of those self-denying virtues is not Christian), *Ash Wednesday* with its tone of humility and self-abnegation, some of the choruses from *The Rock,* among other things, the discovery of this idea in Grim might have been extremely significant. As it is, the occurrence of the idea in the original narrative was merely fortuitous for Eliot.

The small detail in the Priests' panic-stricken plea for Becket to fly, 'Up the stair. To the roof. To the crypt,' is found in William fitz Stephen's account. He suggests that Becket might easily have fled: 'the crypt was near at hand . . . he might have climbed by a spiral staircase to the arched chambers in the roof of the church.'

A further comment by Grim on Becket's behaviour in face of death —'The righteous shall be as bold as a lion and without fear'—reappears in the play:

> It is the just man who
> Like a bold lion, should be without fear.

It may also have provided Eliot with the controlling thought for the Knights' drunken chant, 'Come down Daniel to the lion's den.' Only a taunt phrased in these terms would demand such a reply from Becket. And so to the end of the section with the murder of the Archbishop, Eliot adhered closely to his authority for the brisk exchanges between Becket and his murderers. The speech reported by Grim—

> 'I, too, am ready to die for my Lord, that in my blood the Church may obtain peace and liberty; but in the name of Almighty God I forbid you to harm any of my men, whether clerk or lay'—

becomes in the play:

> For my Lord I am now ready to die,
> That His Church may have peace and liberty.
> Do with me as you will, to your hurt and shame;
> But none of my people, in God's name,
> Whether layman or clerk, shall you touch.
> This I forbid.

The final exchange between Becket and fitz Urse (Eliot's First Knight) is a faithful record of the facts, as are Becket's last words—he 'commended his cause and that of the Church to God and St. Mary and the blessed martyr, St. Denys'—which Eliot slightly extends by the traditional phrasing of the liturgy.

All the evidence is not given here, but it is clear enough that Eliot uses extensively his authoritative source—and Professor Douglas claims Grim as the best authority—selecting from it ideas, phrases, and whole speeches to forward the action and develop the theme of his play. The selection does not seem to have been a difficult task. While Eliot is not a hero-worshipper of Becket as Grim was, both men approach the event of Becket's death from much the same angle. Grim sees Becket as 'a man of God,' 'Christ's champion,' 'Christ's doughty champion,' and if one interprets these descriptive titles to mean that Becket was an advocate for the religious attitude to life, a man, who has 'lost his will in the will of God' and whose single purpose is sacrifice to God's overriding purpose, in opposition to the man-centred creed of Secularism concerned with 'morals only of a collective nature'—then Eliot's attitude is not very different from Grim's. That Eliot can so readily use Grim's phrases—and not only those which are primarily of narrative value—surely supports this claim. Neither, perhaps, was the problem of transposing prose statements into verse very troublesome. In *Poetry and Drama,* while disclaiming any permanent discovery from his experiments in *Murder in the Cathedral,* Eliot says he had in mind 'the versification of *Everyman.*' The tradition behind the idiom of *Everyman* is clearly biblical, and the same tradition lies behind Grim's (Latin) language. The idiom of the two languages being so nearly identical must undoubtedly have diminished Eliot's difficulty in this respect. . . .

THE CHORUS

David E. Jones

In a talk broadcast in the year after the first production of *Murder in the Cathedral,* Eliot remarked that:

'in making use of [the chorus] we do not aim to *copy* Greek drama. There is a good deal about the Greek theatre that we do not know, and never shall know. But we know that some of its conventions cannot be ours. The characters frequently talk too long; the chorus has too much to say and holds up the action; usually not enough happens; and the Greek notion of climax is not ours. But the chorus has always fundamentally

From "'Murder in the Cathedral' (*1935*)," in The Plays of T. S. Eliot by *David E. Jones* (London: Routledge & Kegan Paul. Second Impression 1961), pp. 52–54. Copyright © 1960 by David E. Jones. Reprinted by permission of the University of Toronto Press, and of Routledge & Kegan Paul.

the same uses. It mediates between the action and the audience; it intensifies the action by projecting its emotional consequences, so that we as the audience see it doubly, by seeing its effect on other people.' [1]

To this end, Eliot restored the full-throated chorus of Greek tragedy after centuries in which it was reduced to a single expositor of the action. (The dramatic poems, like those of Milton and Swinburne, in which the full chorus was used were plays for reading rather than performance.) He has, in fact, gone back to the fountainhead of European drama and restored the Aeschylean form.[2] He has used the chorus to open out the action into its full significance, as nobody else has done since Aeschylus.

But Eliot has not just copied Aeschylus; he has given the chorus a new significance in the light of the Christian dispensation. In Aeschylus the chorus has a character of its own—it consists of elders of Argos, or libation bearers, or some such personages—but for the most part it is just the author's mouthpiece, his principal means of conveying his vision of the significance of the action. In *Murder in the Cathedral* the chorus is much farther individualized. This is due less perhaps to the influence of naturalism and the modern emphasis on individuality than to the implications of Christianity, with its simultaneous emphasis on the precious uniqueness of the individual and the importance of spiritual community. The chorus represents, in effect, the great mass of individuals which Christ came to save: 'we acknowledge ourselves as type of the common man . . .' (p. 87). The martyrdom of Becket is likewise on their behalf. The choruses embody their experience, rather than the author's view of the action. Of course, they speak with his fullness of utterance, not with the limited idiom of real 'scrubbers and sweepers.' But this 'discrepancy' is not far removed from the normal convention of dramatic poetry; what difference there is, can be largely accounted for in terms of the convention of communal speech. They are giving expression to communal feeling, which usually runs deeper than individual feeling, though it is not usually as articulate. The articulateness is poetic illumination, differing from the normal convention of dramatic poetry only in degree.

A theory of the origin of tragedy which was much discussed in the earlier part of the century was that of the Cambridge anthropologists, who thought they had discovered it in the rites of mystery religions

---

[1] 'The Need for Poetic Drama,' *The Listener*, 25 November, 1936, p. 995.
[2] In his essay 'Four Elizabethan Dramatists' Eliot defines his admiration of Aeschylus—and, incidentally, of *Everyman* (*Selected Essays*, Faber and Faber, third enlarged edition, 1951, p. 111).

representing the passion of a god, his death and rebirth, by which the yearly cycle of the disappearance of the seed into the ground and its re-emergence as new life in the spring was assured. Eliot had already used a seasonal myth as the basis of *The Waste Land* and shown his awareness of the parallel with the Christian story of Easter. It may, however, have been the work of the Cambridge anthropologists which suggested to him the possibility of reinforcing the theological pattern by the pattern of myth in *Murder in the Cathedral*.[3]

The fusion of these elements of Christian drama of the Middle Ages with the pre-Christian drama of the Greeks yielded a highly original form. Although nearer to Aeschylean tragedy than to any intervening form, it has been perfectly adapted to Christian theology and is very much of its time. Milton's adaptation of the Greek form to a Biblical theme is a less radical transformation, for all its touches of the baroque. Eliot's work is nearer the stylization of the Byzantine. Yet it has also a functional simplicity which is peculiarly twentieth-century. It resembles certain of the vocal works of Stravinsky more than anything in English dramatic art.

[3] That Eliot was acquainted with the work of Harrison and Cornford, we know from *Selected Essays,* pp. 44 and 62.

The Priests

E. Martin Browne

. . . It is worth noticing that the demands of characterization, limited though they are in this play, are much more subtly fulfilled than may at first be obvious. Take the Priests as examples. They are numbered One, Two and Three; and at a first reading might appear to differ in no more than their numbers. But try giving a speech of Number One to Number Three, and you will quickly find out that they are people of strongly marked character, each of whose speeches belongs to the designated speaker and no one else. Number One is elderly, worldly-

From "*The Dramatic Verse of T. S. Eliot,*" in T. S. Eliot, A Symposium, *Richard March and Tambimuttu,* compilers *(Chicago, Illinois: Henry Regnery Company, 1949). All rights reserved. First published in the United States of America by Henry Regnery Company 1949. Reprinted by permission of the author and the Henry Regnery Company.*

wise, with good manners, fond of his food. . . . Number Two is younger, aggressively loyal, efficient . . . and Number Three is the still, deep thinker who sees the end of things. . . . It is he who at last pronounces the epitaph on the Knights:

Go, weak, sad men, lost, erring souls, homeless in earth or heaven. . . .

BLESSED THOMAS

Carol H. Smith

. . . On the surface level which has been described, *Murder in the Cathedral* is a stylized dramatization of the historical situation of the martyrdom of Thomas Becket presented both as a psychological study of the saint and at the same time as a portrayal of the twelfth-century power struggle of church and state made applicable to the modern world.

But, in addition to the surface level, there is another level of meaning beneath the surface which shows the play to be a development of the dramatic theory evolved earlier and exemplified by *Sweeney Agonistes*. Eliot's treatment of the second level of meaning in *Murder in the Cathedral*, however, introduces an important modification of his use of Cornford's ritual scheme in the earlier play. Eliot kept the basic formulations of the ur-drama but he cast the murdered god in the role of Christ and developed the ritual sequence of events to conform to the Christian interpretation of that pattern in the Biblical lore surrounding Christ's Crucifixion and Resurrection.[1]

The playwright integrates this underlying level of meaning with the surface events by constructing an elaborate dramatic analogy between the martyr and Christ, both of whom are portrayed as divine and sin-laden scapegoats who are mutilated and brought back to renewed life.

From "The Rock *and* Murder in the Cathedral," *in* T. S. Eliot's Dramatic Theory and Practice: From *Sweeney Agonistes* to *The Elder Statesman* (*Princeton: Princeton University Press, 1963*), *pp. 104–109. Copyright © 1963 by Princeton University Press. Reprinted by permission of Princeton University Press.*

[1] For a discussion of the ritual qualifications for the hero and their application to Christ's life see Lord Raglan, *The Hero: A Study in Tradition, Myth, and Drama* (New York: Oxford University Press, 1937), pp. 178–208, and Herbert Weisinger, *Tragedy and the Paradox of the Fortunate Fall* (London: Routledge and Kegan Paul, 1953).

While the martyr as the type of Christ[2] and the presence of elements from the ritual drama[3] have been noted, I believe that neither the completeness of the analogy nor the connection between the theme and the ritual plot has been fully recognized.

Thomas, himself, makes clear the analogy between the martyr and Christ in his Christmas sermon:

"I wish only that you should ponder and meditate the deep meaning and mystery of our masses of Christmas Day. For whenever Mass is said, we re-enact the Passion and Death of Our Lord; and on this Christmas Day we do this in celebration of His Birth. So that at the same moment we rejoice in His coming for the salvation of men, and offer again to God His Body and Blood in sacrifice, oblation and satisfaction for the sins of the whole world.

Not only do we at the feast of Christmas celebrate at once Our Lord's Birth and His Death: but on the next day we celebrate the martyrdom of His first martyr, the blessed Stephen. Is it an accident, do you think, that the day of the first martyr follows immediately the day of the Birth of Christ? By no means. Just as we rejoice and mourn at once, in the Birth and in the Passion of Our Lord; so also, in a smaller figure, we both rejoice and mourn in the death of martyrs. We mourn, for the sins of the world that has martyred them; we rejoice, that another soul is numbered among the Saints in Heaven, for the glory of God and for the salvation of men." [4]

The first part of the play, in which Thomas is visited by the Tempters, may thus be viewed as symbolic of Christ's Temptation and the second part, in which Thomas' martyrdom is enacted, as the Passion, Death, and Resurrection of Christ. The opening chorus establishes the analogy between the women drawn to the Cathedral at the Christmas season because of their presentiment of a tremendous event to be enacted and the birth of Christ, in such lines as: "The New Year waits, destiny waits for the coming," and "Shall the Son of Man be born again in the litter of scorn?" The imagery used by the women to express their fear of the coming of life is similar to that used in the opening of *The Waste Land.*

[2] See, for example, Grover Smith, *T. S. Eliot's Poetry and Plays: A Study in Sources and Meaning* (Chicago, Illinois: The University of Chicago Press, 1956), p. 186.

[3] Both David E. Jones, *The Plays of T. S. Eliot* (London: Routledge & Kegan Paul, 1960), pp. 53–54, and Francis Fergusson, *The Idea of a Theater* (Princeton, New Jersey: Princeton University Press, 1949), pp. 211–13, mention the presence of the ritual structure.

[4] T. S. Eliot, *The Complete Poems and Plays: 1909–1950* (New York: Harcourt, Brace and Company, 1952), pp. 198–99.

The Herald's description of the coming of the Archbishop into the city echoes Christ's triumphal entry into Jerusalem, even to the colt mentioned in Matthew and Luke and the strewing of garments and branches in Matthew; at the same time it develops the analogy to the procession of Phales mentioned by Cornford and Murray.

Thomas' four temptations, though not exactly analogous to Christ's in the desert, are close enough to be convincing if one equates the Devil's request that Christ turn the stones into bread with the First Tempter's appeal to Thomas' appetites, the Devil's offer of the kingdoms of the world with the inducements of the Second and Third Tempters, and the Devil's attempt to make Christ throw himself down from the pinnacle in order to prove his divinity with the Fourth Tempter's appeal to Thomas' pride in willing martyrdom. In addition, just as Christ's Sermon on the Mount follows immediately Christ's temptation in Matthew, so the Christmas sermon of Thomas follows *his* temptation.

Part II contains the agon of the drama, the struggle of the sin-laden god-figure, in the person of the Archbishop, with his antagonists. It develops, at the same time, several similarities between the Gospel accounts of Christ's passion and Thomas' martyrdom. The most obvious analogy is between the Crucifixion of Christ and the murder of Thomas by the jealous seekers after power in this world, and the acceptance of death by both Christ and the martyr as a part of God's design for the redemption of mankind. But other similarities also exist: for example, the supper the Priests mention in the beginning of Part II may be meant to represent both the Last Supper and the ritual feast, and the Knights' false accusations against Thomas may be intended to suggest both the trial of Christ and the battle of insults engaged in by the god and his antagonist.

Thomas' triumphant statement, just before his death, on the purification of blood,

> I am a priest,
> A Christian, saved by the blood of Christ,
> Ready to suffer with my blood.
> This is the sign of the Church always,
> The sign of blood. Blood for blood.
> His blood given to buy my life,
> My blood given to pay for His death,
> My death for His death,[5]

[5] Ibid., p. 213.

emphasizes the reciprocity between Christ's and the martyr's death. Christ shed his blood for the remission of human sin and the martyr, in return, sheds his blood both in repayment for and in re-enactment of Christ's sacrifice. Blood is a multiple symbol in the play and the women view it differently. To them it is symbolic of their blood-guilt in the shedding of the saint's, and by analogy Christ's, blood:

The land is foul, the water is foul, our beasts and ourselves defiled with blood. A rain of blood has blinded my eyes. Where is England? where is Kent? where is Canterbury?

O far far far far in the past; and I wander in a land of barren boughs: if I break them, they bleed; I wander in a land of dry stones: if I touch them they bleed.[6]

The theme of blood-guilt is also present in Matthew's version of Pilate's offer to give Christ to the multitude:

"He [Pilate] took water, and washed his hands before the multitude, saying, I am innocent of the blood of this just person: see ye to it. Then answered all the people, and said, His blood be on us, and on our children." [7]

The rain of blood and other lines in the same chorus, including "Night stay with us, stop sun, hold season, let the day not come, let the spring not come," suggest the darkness and earthquake which occurred at Christ's death. The references in the women's chorus to the stones leading to Dante's river of Blood and to the bleeding boughs of the Suicides in the *Inferno* indicate that though the women do not yet realize it, the blood they interpret only as a sign of their terrible guilt will bring them to a penitential state of grace. Thus the death of the martyr and of Christ includes both good and evil, guilt and glory, just as the killing of the god represents both sin and necessity to primitive worshippers.

The concluding lines of the play emphasize a final correspondence between the Savior and the saint. The women, acknowledging their sin, chant:

Lord, have mercy upon us.
Christ, have mercy upon us.
Lord, have mercy upon us.
Blessed Thomas, pray for us.[8]

The Resurrection of Christ is paralleled by the entrance of Thomas

[6] Ibid., p. 214.
[7] Matt. 27:24–25.
[8] Eliot, *Complete Poems and Plays*, p. 221.

into the ranks of sainthood, and thus the women can pray to both
Christ and Thomas for mercy and intercession.[9] . . .

[9] Another aspect of the ritual scheme as described by Cornford and Murray which
appears in the play is the winning over of the chorus by the protagonist. It is duplicated in *Murder in the Cathedral* by the women's gradual acceptance of their place
in the martyr's triumph. There may also be a connection between Eliot's use of the
turning wheel symbolism and the spiritual doctor who revives the god; Grover
Smith traces the wheel-point imagery to Aristotle's *De Anima* and the physician-
patient theme to another of Aristotle's treatises, *De Generatione et Corruptione*—
both of which are treatments of God as unsuffering "first-mover" (*T. S. Eliot's Poetry
and Plays*, p. 188).

BECKET AS JOB

Robert N. Shorter

In "The Three Voices of Poetry" T. S. Eliot says that the plot of
Murder in the Cathedral "had the drawback . . . of presenting only
one dominant character; and what dramatic conflict there is takes place
within the mind of that character." Later in the same essay Eliot risks
the generalization, admittedly rather sweeping, that "character is created and made real only in action, a communication between imaginary
people." [1] The success of *Murder in the Cathedral* would therefore
seem to depend on Eliot's ability to create Thomas Becket's "reality"
through dramatic communication. Yet toward the end of Part I Becket
remains silent as the Women of Canterbury, the four Tempters, and
the Priests speak in combined chorus, and during this silence occurs the
decision by which he overcomes his self-destructive pride and resolves
his conflict. Following the chorus, Becket says he has found the right
reason for the "right deed" of martyrdom.[2] Since the critical and dramatic effect of Becket within the play depends on the believability of

"*Becket as Job: T. S. Eliot's* Murder in the Cathedral" *by Robert N. Shorter. From*
The South Atlantic Quarterly, *LXVII, 4 (Autumn 1968), 627–35. Copyright © 1968
by* The South Atlantic Quarterly. *Reprinted by permission of the author and the
journal.*

[1] *On Poetry and Poets* (New York, 1957), pp. 99, 104.
[2] This point is discussed in more detail by Hugh Kenner, *The Invisible Poet: T. S.
Eliot* (New York, 1959), p. 280.

his spiritual decision, this period of silence is the most crucial portion of the play.[3]

In the Christmas Sermon Interlude Becket cites the humility of the Saint, which is in direct contrast to the pride of the false martyr: "Saints are most high, having made themselves most low . . ." through submission to God's will.[4] This characterization of the true martyr focuses the dramatic problem of Part I, for it accords, at least superficially, with the Fourth Tempter's appeal to Thomas: "Make yourself the lowest / On earth, to be high in heaven." Becket's pride, his self-conscious seeking of martyrdom, would lead to his death; and his humility, his submission to the will of God, leads to his death. Different motivations do not issue in different overt results, and Becket's moment of decision cannot be fully exhibited through action.[5]

The key to understanding the moment of decision is to recognize the analogy between Becket and Job, an analogy which has been suggested, but not developed, by Grover Smith in *T. S. Eliot's Poetry and Plays,* in which he says "Eliot could have borrowed his four Tempters from Job. . . ."[6] A comparison of *Murder in the Cathedral* and the Book of Job validates Smith's suggestion: the four Tempters of Becket do parallel the four Comforters of Job, and Becket in Part I is a Job-like figure. The analogy between Becket and Job reveals that the problems of Becket's decision, both critical and dramatic, are apparent rather than real, and that *Murder in the Cathedral* is dramatically successful.

An alternate suggestion by some critics is to find a parallel between Becket and Christ, specifically a parallel between the Tempters of Becket and the temptations of Christ.[7] However, this analogy exposes the apparent dramatic defect at the heart of Eliot's play, because it assumes that Becket returns from France as a Christ-figure and therefore does not develop through conflict embodied in the actual dramatic presentation. Becket cannot be a Christ-figure in the temptation scene of Part I because of differences too significant to overlook between the

---

[3] The apparently undramatic quality of the silence has led some critics to regard the play as ultimately a dramatic failure; for example, see Helen Gardner, *The Art of T. S. Eliot* (New York, 1950), pp. 135–139.

[4] References are to the edition of the play contained in T. S. Eliot, *The Complete Poems and Plays* (New York, n. d.).

[5] In "The Three Voices of Poetry" Eliot distinguishes drama as "essentially an action exhibited to an audience" (p. 105).

[6] Chicago, 1956, p. 185. As far as I know, the implications of this possibility have never been traced.

[7] Two such attempts are those by William R. Mueller, "*Murder in the Cathedral:* An Imitation of Christ," *Religion in Life*, XXVII (1958), 414; and Carol H. Smith, *T. S. Eliot's Dramatic Theory and Practice* (Princeton, 1963), pp. 106–107.

temptations of Becket and Christ, and between Becket's Tempters themselves.

Most obviously, Becket faces four, not three temptations. Had Eliot intended an analogy with Christ, he could have omitted the Third Tempter, representative of the barons, without serious damage to the scene, and without sacrificing the historical necessity of four Knights in Part II. An even more important difference is the fact that Christ in the wilderness faced and overcame genuine temptations; were they not genuine, they would not be meaningful. Becket's first three Tempters, the past history of his transition from secular to religious, are easily dismissed because they have long since been overcome, and only the Fourth Tempter presents a genuine challenge to Becket. The difference between the first three Tempters and the Fourth Tempter is the difference between the past and present of Becket himself, and is emphasized by a further, and most important, difference: Becket *expects* three Tempters. "I am an unexpected visitor," says the Third Tempter, and Becket coolly replies, "I expected you." When the Fourth Tempter enters with mocking applause for Becket's dismissal of the first three, Becket's composure is shaken: "Who are you? I expected / Three visitors, not four."

Becket's expectation of the Third Tempter, twice emphasized by Eliot, reveals that Becket *regards himself* as a Christ-figure, and that therefore, at this point in the play, he is *not* a Christ-figure. Becket's presumptive attitude dramatically communicates the pride which initially brings him back to Canterbury, and if he is to become truly Christlike in his martyrdom, he can do so only as a result of the developing action of the play. That is, the spiritual decision which Becket makes during his silence toward the end of Part I must be a consequence of the dramatic action presented on stage, rather than an extra-dramatic assumption unrelated to the developing action. Seeing himself as a Christ-figure, Becket has refused to subordinate himself even to God, and thus the entrance of the unexpected fourth visitor defines exactly for Becket his state of mortal sin, and reduces him to despair. The four Tempters of Part I do not reveal Becket as parallel to Christ; rather they discover the spiritual chasm between Becket and Christ at this point in the play.

The analogy in Part I of *Murder in the Cathedral* between Becket and Job is, in contrast to that between Becket and Christ, critically and dramatically illuminating. Job and Becket have suffered as a result of devotion to God; both, as they respond to the first three Comforters and to the first three Tempters, are self-righteous in their presumption of sinlessness; both are brought through unexpected fourth visitors to recognize their sin; both are saved from the brink of damnation; both Job and Beckett are found acceptable in the sight of God. The analogy further suggests what happens within Becket during his period of silence in which he negates his own will in order to overcome his despair: he receives an illumination corresponding to the voice of God speaking to Job out of the whirlwind.

Job is able to dismiss his first three Comforters as "physicians of no value" because "thou writest bitter things against me, and makest me to possess the iniquities of my youth" (13:26). Becket is able to dismiss his first three Tempters because they are all from his past, and can offer him only the iniquities of his spiritual youth. To the First Tempter's recall of worldly pleasures Becket says, "You come twenty years too late." When the Second Tempter offers secular power through submission to the King, Becket replies:

> I *was* the King, his arm, his better reason.
> But what was once exaltation
> Would now be only mean descent.

In rejecting the "happy coalition / Of intelligent interests" offered by the Third Tempter, Becket asks: "Shall I who ruled like an eagle over doves / Now take the shape of a wolf among wolves?" In respect to these temptations Becket is sinless, and he is self-righteous. His easy rejection of the first three Tempters expresses his drive for spiritual power, and in this sense his own lips testify against him; when Job in his self-righteousness rejects the first Comforter, the latter says to him: "Thine own mouth condemneth thee, and not I: yea, thine own lips testify against thee" (15:6). Job later says: "And be it indeed that I have erred, mine error remaineth with myself" (19:4). When the Third Tempter leaves, Becket's parting remark is: "But if I break, I must break myself alone." The sin of both Becket and Job, which they must recognize before they can overcome it, is the self-imposed, self-damning sin of pride.

When the first three Comforters have no effect on Job, "these three men ceased to answer Job, because he was righteous in his own eyes. Then was kindled the wrath of Elihu the son of Barachel the Buzite, of the kindred of Ram: against Job was his wrath kindled, because he justified himself rather than God" (32:1–2). This is the first mention in the Book of Job of Elihu. Coming as it does approximately three-quarters through the Book, this entry of the fourth Comforter is "unexpected," just as the entry of the Fourth Tempter in *Murder in the Cathedral* is unexpected. Elihu in his wrath tells Job: "Behold, in this thou art not just: I will answer thee, that God is greater than man"

(33:12). Becket, in the self-conscious equation of himself with Christ, has forgotten that God is greater than man; in seeking martyrdom through his self-justified will Becket has arrogated the direction of God's purpose.

Job's silence before Elihu's accusation prompts Elihu to say "hold thy peace, and I shall teach thee wisdom" (33:33), because "Job hath spoken without knowledge, and his words were without wisdom" (34:35). Elihu then summarizes the core of spiritual wisdom, the basis for submission to God: "Touching the Almighty, we cannot find him out . . ." (37:23). Only by accepting human limitation as a corrective to pride can man achieve wisdom. In *Murder in the Cathedral* Becket implicitly defines wisdom by characterizing the fool:

> Only
> The fool, fixed in his folly, may think
> He can turn the wheel on which he turns.

Becket, on the perimeter of the wheel whose axis is God, thinks to turn the wheel on which he turns.[8] Like Job, Becket has embraced the evil of pride by refusing to accept his human limitation.

After Elihu has finished accusing Job, God speaks directly to Job out of the whirlwind and confirms what Elihu has said: man cannot understand or effect God's purpose. Job's self-righteousness is shattered and he is reduced to silence: "Behold, I am vile; what shall I answer thee?" (40:4). Job's recognition and silent acceptance of his sin are paralleled in *Murder in the Cathedral* by Becket's last speech in response to the Fourth Tempter:

> Is there no way, in my soul's sickness,
> Does not lead to damnation in pride?
> I well know that these temptations
> Mean present vanity and future torment.
> Can sinful pride be driven out
> Only by more sinful? Can I neither act
>   nor suffer
> Without perdition?

Becket can no longer self-righteously answer his Tempters. His questioning clearly reveals his recognition of his "sinful pride," and, like Job, he lapses into silent acceptance.

God continues to speak to Job after Job's recognition of his sin, and

---

[8] Eliot's use of the wheel as image is examined in detail by Louis L. Martz, "The Wheel and the Point: Aspects of Imagery and Theme in Eliot's Later Poetry," *T. S. Eliot: A Selected Critique*, ed. Leonard Unger (New York, 1948), pp. 444–462.

Job is finally brought to full repentance: "I abhor myself, and repent in dust and ashes" (42:6). With Job's repentance comes his reward from God, which, though manifested by a return to physical and economic prosperity, is spiritual. Elihu has said to Job that God "looketh upon men, and if any say, I have sinned, and perverted that which was right, and it profited me not; He will deliver his soul from going into the pit, and his life shall see the light" (33:27–28). Thomas Becket's soul has come close to the pit of "damnation in pride." His last speech in Part I shows his genuine repentance for his pride, and the Christmas Sermon shows that he now serves God instead of self. The full confirmation that Becket's repentance makes him acceptable in the sight of God comes with his spiritual reward of Sainthood.

The parallel between Becket and Job provides a critical understanding for the most crucial point in *Murder in the Cathedral*—Becket's period of silence toward the close of Part I. During his silence Becket has a spiritual illumination corresponding to God's speaking to Job out of the whirlwind. God's voice does not speak aloud to Becket; Eliot chose not to present—even for a presumably religious audience at the festival of Canterbury—God as *dramatis persona*. Rather he chose the combined chorus of the Women of Canterbury, the Tempters, and the Priests to dramatize the whirlwind and to imply the voice of God.

In "Poetry and Drama," in which he discusses the problems he faced in *Murder in the Cathedral* and his attempted solutions, Eliot says:

> It seems to me that beyond the nameable, classifiable emotions and motives of our conscious life when directed towards action—the part of life which prose drama is wholly adequate to express—there is a fringe of indefinite extent, of feeling which we can only detect, so to speak, out of the corner of the eye and can never completely focus; of feeling of which we are only aware in a kind of temporary detachment from action. . . . This peculiar range of sensibility can be expressed by dramatic poetry, at its moments of greatest intensity.[9]

Becket's silence is what Eliot calls a "temporary detachment from action," during which Becket experiences emotions as intense as man is capable of.[10] Since Eliot was unable to dramatize through action directly involving Becket the resolution of Becket's spiritual struggle, the experience cannot be directly focused on and therefore must be detected "out of the corner of the eye" of the combined chorus which speaks during Becket's silence. Previously in "Poetry and Drama" Eliot has said, "if there prove to be scenes which we cannot put in verse, we

[9] *On Poetry and Poets*, p. 93.

[10] Elizabeth Drew discusses this kind of experience as "detachment from the world of objective reality," in *T. S. Eliot: The Design of His Poetry* (New York, 1949), p. 12.

must either develop our verse, or avoid having to introduce such scenes" (p. 78). In one important sense Eliot was unable to "put in verse" the resolution within Becket, yet he could not "avoid having to introduce" the scene of Becket's silence, for, without it, Becket's martyrdom would seem "Senseless self-slaughter of a lunatic" (*Murder in the Cathedral*, Part I). Eliot's only alternative was to develop his verse. In "Poetry and Drama" Eliot says of the Women of Canterbury, "The use of a chorus strengthened the power, and concealed the defects of my theatrical technique" (p. 86). The combined chorus of Women, Tempters, and Priests—the only instance in the play of a combined chorus of more than one set of characters—triples the power and conceals the major defect, if such it be, of the play. Becket's silence reflects his detachment; the chorus reflects his struggle.

The combined chorus, with its talk of "restless movement," man's life as "a cheat and a disappointment," and "the stifling scent of despair," establishes a mood appropriate to Becket's struggle even if it cannot directly embody that struggle. But it does more than just conceal a dramatic defect: it corresponds to and mirrors Becket's internal conflict, and provides him with the right reason for martyrdom. Admittedly the chorus speaks on the secular level of man's physical life on earth, a life which seeks to avoid rather than to encounter God. But all their remarks are ambiguous; there is not one specific reference which would prevent a spiritual interpretation of what they say. Becket in response to the chorus can learn a lesson far transcending the intended meaning and enabling him to see clearly his way toward God.

The Women initially establish the atmosphere, illustrated by the sentence, "The earth is heaving the parturition of issue of hell." Then the Tempters speak of Becket:

> This man is obstinate, blind, intent
> On self-destruction,
> Passing from deception to deception,
> From grandeur to grandeur to final illusion,
> Lost in the wonder of his own greatness,
> The enemy of society, enemy of himself.

Then the three Priests say to Becket, "do not fight the intractable tide," presumably of secular opposition. The general statement of the Priests introduces for the first time the counsel of submission, which for Becket must be spiritual. Next the Women, Priests, and Tempters alternate single lines, all to the effect that man can neither prevent nor anticipate death; following the Priests' implication of submission, these lines tell Becket that he cannot will his own death, but must accept it when-

ever and however it comes. Finally the Women, in the long final portion of the chorus, speak of the "living and partly living" made bearable only by God-given hope. But now, they say, "a new terror has soiled us," the absence of reason or hope. They then conclude with a direct appeal to Becket: "O Thomas Archbishop, save us, save us, save yourself that we may be saved; / Destroy yourself and we are destroyed."

The movement of the combined chorus mirrors the stages of Becket's struggle: hellish despair; recognition of his will to self-destruction; the idea of submission; the relinquishing of the will to death; motivation for submission in saving the Women. The tumultuous effect of the combined chorus itself has a whirlwind quality, and the ambiguous content implies for Becket the same lesson that Job learned directly from God.

The analogy between Becket and Job is valid only in Part I of *Murder in the Cathedral,* when Becket undergoes his temptation. Though both Becket and Job are rewarded for their submission to God, Job is not a Christian martyr. Becket is—yet he becomes so only in the course of the play. At the conclusion of Part I he is freed from pride, and as a result in Part II achieves a martyrdom which, as defined in the Christmas Sermon, elevates him to the level of a true Christ-figure. But it remains the initial parallel with Job which explains Becket's struggle and achievement in overcoming his temptation, and which enabled Eliot successfully to create Thomas Becket's spiritual reality through dramatic action.

THOMAS'S TEMPTATION

H. Z. Maccoby

Why does the Fourth Tempter end his Temptation by repeating to Thomas his own words, "You know and do not know what it is to act or suffer . . . "? Commentators seem to agree that this is some kind of taunt or sneer. The words are "flung back at him" (D. E. Jones).[1] "The advice he has given is turned against him" (Nevill Coghill).[2] On this in-

From "Two Notes on 'Murder in the Cathedral'" by H. Z. Maccoby. From Notes and Queries, *XIV (July, 1967), 253–55. Copyright © 1967 by H. Z. Maccoby. Reprinted by permission of the author and the journal.*

[1] *The Plays of T. S. Eliot* (Routledge, 1960).
[2] *Murder in the Cathedral,* ed. N. Coghill (Faber Educational Books, 1965).

terpretation, the whole speech is to be delivered in tones of savage irony. Thomas's analysis of action has been refuted by the revelation that disinterested action is impossible; even to give one's wholehearted and disinterested assent to God's pre-ordained pattern is beyond the capacity of a human being, whose aspirations towards saintliness are only a particularly deadly form of selfregard. Alternatively, the Tempter is taunting Thomas about his failure to understand and live up to his own words (D. E. Jones). This is the "final turn of the screw".

These interpretations seem to me implausible. It would be very difficult, perhaps impossible, for the actor to deliver the speech effectively in the way described. The rhythms are too calm and measured to be given the required ironic twist, and in any case the speech is too long for such a tone to be sustained. A receptive reading of the whole passage in the play leaves the conviction that, on the contrary, the repetition of this profound and central speech is intended as a kind of summing-up of the lesson of the Fourth Temptation. The Tempter is not taunting but teaching, not sneering but comforting, just as Thomas was comforting the women of Canterbury when he first spoke the same words. This is not to deny that there is a touch of irony in the situation; for the Tempter is teaching Thomas something that he thought he knew already. The irony is not an expression of vindictiveness, nor does it lie in any allegation of falsehood in the words themselves. It arises simply from the fact that Thomas, the teacher, is now the pupil. There is especial irony in the phrase, "You know and do not know. . . ." When Thomas had applied similar words to the women of Canterbury, there had been a little condescension in his assertion that the women had an instinctive grasp of profundities which they were unable to put into articulate form. Now it has become clear that Thomas has been able to put into articulate form something of which so far he has had no instinctive grasp. He too "knows and does not know," but he knows what the women of Canterbury do not know, and does not know what they know.

What kind of person does this make the Fourth Tempter? There are several indications that he is not a mere seducer from virtue but has a deeper role. This role is to make Thomas face his own repressed motives in all their ugliness and so achieve purification from them. The Tempter speaks not as one putting before Thomas seductive pleasure and glory, but as one laying bare to the horrified Thomas the vulgarity of his own desires. Does the Fourth Tempter really think that he is *tempting* Thomas by offering him the pleasure of seeing "far off below you, where the gulf is fixed, / Your persecutors, in timeless torment . . . "? Or is he not rather forcing Thomas to realize the baseness of his own secret vision of glory? (This particular pleasure, as Eliot un-doubtedly knew, was one much prized by Tertullian and other authori-ties, and the historical Thomas would perhaps not have found it disreputable.) The essence of the kind of vainglorious, sadistic day-dreaming exposed in the Fourth Temptation is that it should not be admitted to full consciousness. Once it is so admitted, and the critical light of the adult moral consciousness allowed to play on it, it immedi-ately loses its force. If the Fourth Tempter had really wished Thomas to be damned in this particular way, it would have served his demonic purposes far better not to have approached him at all. The approach of the Fourth Tempter is, in fact, the beginning of Thomas's salvation.

Yet there is also enough in the presentation of the Fourth Tempter to make him appear to be after all the Evil One, Satan himself. He says, "I offer what you desire. I ask / What you have to give." Here he speaks the language of Mephistopheles to Faust. While the first three Tempt-ers are solid human beings, individually characterized, the Fourth Tempter is a supernatural being, bringing with him an aura of dread and fascination. (It is of course possible to regard all four Tempters as embodiments of aspects of Thomas's own mind; but once they have been so embodied we must take them on their own dramatic terms. Eliot's first conception of the first three Tempters was even more solidly characterized. He toned down the realism of their presentation, but still left them recognizable human beings.)

The solution to the paradox, I suggest, is that Eliot has hit on a con-ception of the Tempter as the servant of God. This is a Jewish rather than a Christian notion. It would be interesting to know how far Eliot had studied the idea in the Jewish sources.[3] No other conception, I think, can do justice to the extraordinary interest and subtley of the Fourth Tempter's role. He forces upon Thomas a loathing which re-veals itself as self-loathing. He tempts him with his own thoughts, which he has been unwilling to acknowledge or avow for what they are, and which only have to be avowed to be rejected. The Fourth Tempter has a grasp of the total situation far beyond that of the other Tempters, who naïvely expect that Thomas will be seduced. It is thus not at all inappropriate that when Thomas, convinced of his own worthlessness, sinks into despair and doubts the possibility of human justification ("Can I neither act nor suffer / Without perdition?"), the Tempter re-

[3] In the Babylonian Talmud (*Baba Bathra* 16a) R. Acha bar Jacob expounds Satan's good intentions in the Job affair, and Satan comes and kisses the Rabbi's knees in gratitude. In the Old Testament, Satan appears in heaven among the "sons of God" (Job, 1). The idea that Satan was responsible for the Fall is not found in the Old Testament. Nor is the story of Satan's rebellion against God.

minds him of the analysis previously made by Thomas himself of the meaning of action and justification. The conviction of sin must precede salvation, and Thomas's despair here corresponds to the despair of the Chorus later in the play, which breaks through their complacency and prepares them for purification. Self-regard, the Tempter is saying, rests ultimately on an overestimation of the power of human action. Thomas is ambitious because he still thinks that his fate is in his own hands, that he can manipulate his promotion in the court of the Heavenly King. The conviction of helplessness accompanies the conviction of sin, and this helplessness is the essential basis for a true exercise of free-will in consenting to God's inevitable plan. This is the point of the Tempter's reminder, and when he makes it, he is revealed as a messenger of God, a comforter and angel, rather than a devil; or, more accurately, he is a devil who is the servant of God, using temptation to awaken men to the knowledge of their own souls.[4]

[4] For a similar ambiguity of role in *The Cocktail Party*, see D. E. Jones, *The Plays of T. S. Eliot*, p. 153. Reilly is the "devil" who is really an angel. The Eumenides, too, in *The Family Reunion*, have a devil-angel role.

THE TEMPTATION OF THE AUDIENCE

David E. Jones

The Knights' apologia for their action is far from being an excrescence, as some critics have suggested. It is an integral part of the play. It is, in effect, the temptation of the audience, corresponding to the temptation of Thomas in Part I, as is subtly indicated by the doubling of the Tempters and the Knights. As we shall see, the second half of the play is concerned largely with the second half of the pattern of martyrdom, the creation of the attitude of acceptance in the great mass of believers. With and through the Chorus, we of the audience are invited to participate in the celebration of the act of martyrdom and to accept the sacrifice of Thomas as made in our behalf. Before we can do this, however, we, like Thomas, must undergo temptation, in our case the temptation to deny the efficacy of his sacrifice and its relevance to us.

Stepping out of their twelfth-century setting, the Knights seek by every means from blandishment to exhortation, cunningly using the techniques of modern political oratory, to make us admit the reasonableness of their action and to acknowledge that we are involved in it, since we have benefited from it.

For the Knights the play is over, and the First Knight suggests 'that you now disperse quietly to your homes' (p. 83). But for most of us in the audience the arguments will have had the opposite effect to that intended by the Knights. We admit that we are implicated in the death of Thomas, but we do not concede the justification of the killing on the grounds argued by the Knights. The benefit we acknowledge is spiritual rather than political and it comes from Thomas's suffering rather than their action. For us, therefore, the play is not over; the effect of Thomas's sacrifice continues. The Priests enter and help us to recover the mood of the martyrdom in a chastened form. From a threnody for the archbishop in the minor key, the recovered verse-form modulates to the major and the great hymn of praise and thanksgiving for the new saint in glory with which the play ends. The pattern of mourning and rejoicing which Thomas distinguished in the death of martyrs, as in the Birth and Passion of Christ, is here fulfilled.[1] By cutting down the historical action to its bare essentials, Eliot has brought 'the eternal design' into stark relief.[2]

[1] Cf. the sermon, *Murder in the Cathedral* (fourth edition, 1938), p. 30.
[2] The sensuous detail excluded from the action of the play returns, however, with the full impact of poetry, in the choruses.

A Shaft of Sunlight

Kristian Smidt

. . . The intensest moments in Eliot's spiritual experience seem to have been those he referred to in a broadcast talk on 'The Significance of Charles Williams' given in 1946, where he said that 'there are pages in [Williams's] novels which describe, with extraordinary precision, the kind of unexplainable experience which many of us have had, once or twice in our lives, and been unable to put into words.'[1] In one of my

From **Poetry and Belief in the Work of T. S. Eliot** by *Kristian Smidt (London: Routledge & Kegan Paul, Ltd., and New York: The Humanities Press, Inc.), pp. 174–79. Copyright © 1961 by Kristian Smidt. Reprinted by permission of the author, Routledge & Kegan Paul, Ltd., and of the Humanities Press, Inc.*

[1] *Listener,* Dec. 19, 1946.

conversations with Mr. Eliot I asked him if he was seeking a spiritual revelation in the *Four Quartets*. He replied that he was not seeking a revelation when writing them, but that he was 'seeking the verbal equivalents for small experiences he had had, and for knowledge derived from reading.' Such 'small experiences' may not be comparable to the ecstasies of the saints, but they are what, for most of us, come closest to the beatific vision.

> For most of us, there is only the unattended
> Moment, the moment in and out of time,
> The distraction fit, lost in a shaft of sunlight,
>   (*The Dry Salvages*, V)

To describe the illumination which comes in these unattended moments, Eliot is fond of using the word 'pattern,' and it is time to find out what exactly he means by this word. I think our best clue will be found in a few lines from his essay on John Marston, which, to my knowledge, have never received the attention they deserve. After giving a number of quotations from Marston's *Sophonisba*, Eliot continues:

> The quotations are intended to exhibit the exceptional consistency of texture of this play. . . . In spite of the tumultuousness of the action, and the ferocity and horror of certain parts of the play, there is an underlying serenity; and as we familiarize ourselves with the play we perceive a pattern behind the pattern into which the characters deliberately involve themselves; the kind of pattern which we perceive in our lives only at rare moments of inattention and detachment, drowsing in sunlight. It is the pattern drawn by what the ancient world called Fate; subtilized by Christianity into mazes of delicate theology; and reduced again by the modern world into crudities of psychological or economic necessity.[2]

The 'shaft of sunlight' has become an almost permanent symbol of such moments of illumination. It is found again in *Murder in the Cathedral*, where the Chorus, still waiting for the unknown to happen, feels that

> Destiny waits in the hand of God, shaping the still unshapen:
> I have seen these things in a shaft of sunlight.

[2] T. S. Eliot, *Selected Essays* (1946 edn.), p. 232.

THE VARIATIONS IN THE TEXT

E. Martin Browne

None of the plays has undergone so many minor textual alterations in the course of successive editions. For Canterbury, the text had to be abbreviated to a set length, and I was obliged to make some mutilations. Meanwhile, Eliot, unable to attend rehearsals, was preparing the first edition for Faber and Faber to be published simultaneously with the Canterbury production. The first edition is thus his own guess at what he wanted in the text without benefit of production experience. The special Canterbury edition was printed locally to be sold at the Festival only and then went out of print. It showed the special cuts, and the re-arrangements necessitated by the varying skills of the actors. Apart from that, however, there are many variations in the Faber printings; and though this is not a book of textual scholarship, it may be valuable to note some of them and the reasons behind them.

One series concerns the division of speeches. When using a group of characters such as the Priests or Knights, an author naturally does not concern himself at first with assigning all his lines to specific individuals. This was mostly done by me in production and adopted into the text afterwards. Thus, in the scene with the Messenger (who, by the way, was originally called Herald in the Greek convention, a title which it would seem better to have retained), the eager questions of the Priests were in the first edition assigned to the First Priest only; in production it was clear that the rest could not stand round and wait speechless while one of their number fired a whole battery of queries, and the division was made as in the subsequent editions. Similarly with their final scene, after the Third Priest's apostrophe to the departed Knights, the others divide the appeal to the new Saint.

The re-assignment of the Knights' lines was made for a different reason. There were a few places in which the author had simply written 'Knights,' leaving me to split the lines up if I liked, or, as with the opening attack on Becket and the final 'Traitor!' cry, to have them spoken in unison. But another consideration arose out of the doubling

From *E. Martin Browne, "Murder in the Cathedral," in* The Making of T. S. Eliot's Plays *(Cambridge: At the University Press, 1969), pp. 72–79. Copyright © 1969 by E. Martin Browne. Reprinted by permission of the author and the publisher.*

of the Tempters with the Knights. The Fourth Tempter, as we have seen, is the most insidious and his influence on Becket's soul is most penetrating. In the temptation of the audience, the same is true of the Fourth Knight, who is employing in reverse the same argument as the Tempter. The Knight asks the audience to believe that Becket has in fact concurred with the Tempter's prompting to will martyrdom for himself to satisfy his own pride, and thus has committed 'suicide.'

In the orginal text, the Fourth Knight takes part with the rest in the violent bullying of Becket that precedes the murder. I soon felt that, with the above interpretation in mind, this was unsuitable. Further, Edward Grim, the eyewitness, tells that 'the fourth knight prevented any from interfering so that the others might freely perpetrate the murder.' [1] It seemed to me that, dramatically, this figure should throughout be a figure of mystery, who while not participating in the violence could be felt to be the influence behind it. So, in the preface to the third edition (1937) Eliot writes:

> At the suggestion of Mr. E. Martin Browne, I have in Part II reassigned most of the lines formerly attributed to the Fourth Knight. When, as was originally intended, the parts of the Tempters are doubled with those of the Knights, the advantages of these alterations should be obvious.

The Knights' exit speech in their first scene was initially weak:

> Priest! monk! and servant! take, hold, detain,
> Restrain this man, in the King's name;
> Or answer with your bodies, if he escape before we come,
> We come for the King's justice, we come again.

As critics were fond of pointing out, the tension was lowered by dividing the confrontation with the Knights into two; but first, this was the historical truth—'then the knights left, vehemently threatening the archbishop and uttering warnings on behalf of the king that he was to be carefully guarded, lest he escape.' [2] Also, the dramatist had some very important things to say before the final onslaught; the two Chorus speeches here, and Becket's own exposition to the Priests, contain some of the most powerful matter, both emotional and intellectual, in the play. But the sheer business of contriving a 'good exit' always troubled Eliot. As late as 31 December 1937, when we were rehearsing for the

---

[1] *Materials for the History of Thomas Becket, Archbishop of Canterbury*, Rolls Series, ed. James Craigie Robertson (London, 1875), II, 31ff. Grim's account is translated by W. H. Hutton in *The English Saints* (Wells, Gardner, Darton & Co., London, 1903), pp. 253–6.

[2] *Materials*, IV, 73.

American tour, he sent me a version which neither of us felt happy
with; and in the end he allowed to stand that which, I think, Ashley
Dukes had suggested some time earlier. It is variously assigned in different editions, but should read thus:

> *First Knight.* Priest! monk! and servant! take, hold, detain,
>   Restrain this man in the King's name,
>   Or answer with your bodies.
> *Second Knight.*   Enough of words.
> *The Three Knights.* We come for the King's justice, we come with swords.
> (*Exeunt*)

It was also Ashley Dukes who had the idea of allowing the First
Knight, as chairman of the 'meeting' after the murder, to characterise
each of the speakers by an introductory phrase. Eliot took this up, and
in his letter of 31 December 1937 he adopts most of Duke's suggestions:

> As for the public meeting. 'My neighbour in the country' seems to me
> quite right. I cannot get anything so concise for Morville. I thought that
> if I could suggest that he was an ambitious young politician, it might
> both sound contemporary and make a good contrast to Traci:
>   'I shall next call upon Hugh de Morville—a name to remember. He
>   is one of our younger statesmen, whom rumour has marked for
>   high office (in the next ministerial shuffle?): there is no one better
>   qualified to expound the constitutional aspect.'
> This is too long, I know.[3] I can't think of any improvement for Brito,
> except that I think 'coming as he does of a family distinguished for its
> *loyalty* to the Church' would be better than *fidelity*.

De Morville's speech underwent a great deal of alteration from the
first version at Canterbury, through the first Faber edition which already incorporated considerable changes made before the text had been
played, to the text which became established. The first edition has:

> The King's aim has been perfectly consistent. During the reign of the
> late Queen Matilda and the irruption of the unhappy usurper Stephen,
> the kingdom was very much divided. Our King saw that the one thing
> needful was to restore order: to curb the excessive powers of local gov-
> ernment, which were usually exercised for selfish and often for seditious
> ends, and to systematise the judiciary. There was utter chaos: there were
> three kinds of justice and three kinds of court: that of the King, that of
> the Bishops, and that of the baronage. I must repeat one point that the
> last speaker has made. While the late archbishop was Chancellor, he
> wholeheartedly supported the King's designs: this is an important point,

[3] It was finally compressed to the single phrase 'who has made a special study of
statecraft and constitutional law.'

which, if necessary, I can substantiate. Now the King intended that Becket, who had proved himself an extremely able administrator—no-one denies that—should unite the offices of Chancellor and Archbishop. No-one would have grudged him that; no-one than he was better qualified to fill at once these two most important posts. Had Becket concurred with the King's wishes . . .

The Canterbury version was more concise, laying stress on the King's reasoning rather than describing the situation he sought to remedy; for instance:

> With a view to assimilating the ecclesiastical jurisdiction to his own, the King designed that Becket should unite the offices . . .

No doubt Eliot learned from watching the scene played that the over-growth printed in the first edition should be pruned; and the final text[4] is a tauter version of this edition, rather than a reversion to Canterbury.

The other differences I wish to note concern Becket himself, and some of them raise interesting questions about ideas in the play. The first occurs in his opening speech.

> They know and do not know, that acting is suffering
> And suffering is action. Neither does the actor suffer . . .

This was the original text; but in rehearsal it became clear that 'acting' and 'actor' in the mouth of a player bore a double meaning; and the lines were altered to:

> They know and do not know, that action is suffering
> And suffering is action. Neither does the agent suffer . . .

The question why a phrase in this speech is omitted by the Fourth Tempter when he throws it back to Thomas has often been asked; it is the kind of question the author never wished to answer, and I can only give my own view. The 'pattern' which is to subsist through action and suffering, in Becket's thinking is the pattern of God's purpose, which is imaged by the wheel turning in symmetrical order around the still centre where God rests. But when the Tempter adopts Becket's words, he interprets the pattern as the mechanical revolution of a wheel which moves automatically, without purpose, round a dead centre; and the lines

                                        for the pattern is the action
         and the suffering

[4] T. S. Eliot, *Collected Plays* (London: Faber & Faber, 1962), p. 50.

cannot apply to this; indeed, if the Tempter used them, he would be denying the interpretation he is putting on the speech.[5]

In the Third Tempter's scene, Becket has, in the first edition only, three lines which never appear again. They are, I believe, based on a recorded saying. The speech dismissing the Tempter runs:

> If the Archbishop cannot trust the Throne,
> He has good cause to trust none but God alone.
> It is not better to be thrown
> To a thousand hungry appetites than to one.
> At a future time this may be shown.
> I ruled once as Chancellor . . .

Among the differences between the Canterbury and the first Faber editions, which as we have seen were in the press at the same time, one of the most considerable is in the penultimate speech of Thomas to the Knights at the end of their first encounter. Here is the Canterbury version:

> It is not I who insult the King
> But those who would have him more than King.
> For there is higher than I or the King.
> I am no traitor, no enemy of the State;
> The King is his own enemy, the State the State's.
> The Law of God is above the law of man,
> The Kingdom of God above the kingdom of man.
> It is not I, Becket from Cheapside,
> It is not against me, Becket, that you strive.
> It is not Becket who pronounces doom,
> But the Law of Christ's Church, the judgment of Rome.

This includes material which re-occurs in the later scene with the Priests; and also some which seems to take colour from the current preoccupation with the danger of dictatorship and the almighty State. In the first Faber edition, this has disappeared, along (perhaps regrettably) with the second line. Here, on the other hand, four lines are added on the theme of Rome's power, which were quickly dropped as weakening the challenge.

> It is not I who insult the King,
> And there is higher than I or the King.
> It is not I, Becket from Cheapside,

[5] See also Nevill Coghill's views on this in the introduction (p. 17) to the educational edition of the play (Faber Educational Books, London, 1965).

It is not against me, Becket, that you strive.
It is not Becket who pronounces doom,
But the Law of Christ's Church, the judgement of Rome.
Go then to Rome, or let Rome come
Here, to you, in the person of her most unworthy son.
Petty politicians in your endless adventure!
Rome alone can absolve those who break Christ's indenture.

The scene with the Priests which falls between the two great choruses,
and in which Becket is taken to vespers, underwent a similar change.
In the Canterbury edition, except for a few extra interjections of fear
from the Priests, the order and text of the speeches are as they were
finally established. But in the first Faber edition Thomas has an extra
speech, and the Priests' replies, to which one has also to be added, are
in a different order:

Priests (*severally*). My Lord, you must not stop here. To the minister.
Through the cloister. No time to waste. They are coming back, armed.
To the altar, to the altar. They are here already. To the sanctuary. They
are breaking in. We can barricade the minster doors. You cannot stay
here. Force him to come. Seize him.
Thomas. All my life they have been coming, these feet. All my life
I have waited. Death will come only when I am worthy,
And if I am worthy, there is no danger.
I have therefore only to make perfect my will.
Priests. My Lord, they are coming. They will break through presently,
You will be killed. Come to the altar.
Thomas. Peace! be quiet! remember where you are, and what is hap-
pening;
No life here is sought for but mine,
And I am not in danger: only near to death.
Priests. Make haste, my Lord. Don't stop here talking. It is not right.
What shall become of us, my Lord, if you are killed; what shall become
of us?
Thomas. That again is another theme
To be developed and resolved in the pattern of time.
It is not for me to run from city to city;
To meet death gladly is only
The only way in which I can defend
The Law of God, the holy canons.
Priests. My Lord, to vespers . . .

There is, I think, no doubt that the shorter version is better; the extra
material probably owed its inclusion rather to being recorded utter-

ances than to the dramatic necessities of the scene. It ends with what is always a crux in production, the hustling of Becket by force into the cathedral; this is vouched for by the eyewitnesses, but is difficult to act, especially with only three Priests, without diminishing Thomas's strength and dignity at a crucial time.

I have left until last the Christmas sermon. The biblical text (Luke 2:14) is given by William Fitzstephen from first-hand knowledge. Eliot originally used it as in the King James version; but afterwards, realising that Becket would have spoken the Vulgate text:

> Gloria in altissmis Deo, et in terra pax hominibus bonae voluntatis

he altered the final words from

> and on earth peace, goodwill towards men

to a translation of the Latin:

> and on earth peace to men of goodwill.

Except for some small differences in wording, the later editions of the play, which may be taken as final, follow closely the Canterbury text. This was worked over in rehearsal by myself and my wife with Speaight, and we consulted the author about many small points, most of which he agreed to and which are now incorporated. But meanwhile, the first Faber edition was in the press with a number of different readings and one considerable expansion. This passage occurs in the following paragraph:

Beloved, we do not think of a martyr simply as a good Christian who has been killed because he is a Christian: for that would be solely to mourn. We do not think of him simply as a good Christian who has been elevated to the company of the Saints: for that would be simply to rejoice: and neither our mourning nor our rejoicing is as the world's is. A Christian martyrdom is no accident. Saints are not made by accident. Still less is a Christian martyrdom the effect of a man's will to become a Saint, as a man by willing and contriving may become a ruler of men. Ambition fortifies the will of man to become ruler over other men: it operates with deception, cajolery and violence, it is the action of impurity upon impurity. Not so in Heaven. A martyr, a saint, is always made by the design of God, for His love of men, to warn them and to lead them, to bring them back to His ways. A martyrdom is never the design of man; for the true martyr is he who has become the instrument of God, who has lost his will in the will of God, not lost it but found it, for he has found freedom in submission to God. The martyr no longer desires anything for himself, not even the glory of martyrdom. So thus as on earth the Church mourns and rejoices at once, in a fashion that the world cannot understand; so in

Heaven the Saints are most high, having made themselves most low, seeing themselves not as we see them, but in the light of the Godhead from which they draw their being.

Here, again, the shorter version is by far the stronger; and it has stood the test of many thousands of performances.

The final paragraph is based on Fitzstephen's account:

he said that they had one martyr-Archbishop, Saint Elphege; it was possible that they would have another in a short time.[6]

and gathers up the thought of the whole into the farewell of Thomas to his people. The eyewitness testimony is that he showed himself deeply moved at this moment; but in playing, so powerful is the emotional effect on the audience that it is better for the actor to make only a restrained suggestion of his feeling. The final line reads in Canterbury:

I would have you ponder no longer on these things now, but at a later time.

But the first Faber edition already contains the alternative which has, rightly I am sure, remained current:

I would have you keep in your hearts these things that I say, and think of them at another time.

[6] *Materials*, III, 130. For translations of extracts see Coghill's edition.

Chronology of Important Dates[1]

	T. S. Eliot	The Age
1888	September 26: T. S. Eliot born in St. Louis, Missouri.	April 15: Death of Matthew Arnold. Tolstoy's *The Power of Darkness* produced. First version of Jarry's *Ubu Roi* performed.
1890		Sir James Frazer's *The Golden Bough* in two volumes, later twelve.
1893		F. H. Bradley's *Appearance and Reality*.
1899		Irish Literary Theatre opens with Yeats's *The Countess Cathleen*.
1900		Sigmund Freud, *The Interpretation of Dreams*.
1905		Einstein advances first theory of relativity.
1906	Enters Harvard (A.B. 1909; M.A. 1910).	Picasso and George Braque evolve Cubism; Dreyfus, sentenced for treason to France in 1884, exonerated. Death of Ibsen.
1907		Bergson's *Creative Evolution*.
1910	At University of Paris; attends Bergson's lectures (1910–1911).	B. Russell and A. N. Whitehead, *Principia Mathematica*. Diaghilev's Ballets Russes produces Stravinsky's *The Firebird*.

[1] The relationship between the two columns of this chronology is not merely fortuitous. The second column contains notice of men, works, and events which throw light on—or are illuminated by—the themes of Eliot's life and poetry and of *Murder in the Cathedral* in particular. The conception of this chronology is my own, but I wish to thank Joseph Hilyard, Richard Noland, and especially Tomas Aczel for going over it and filling some glaring gaps.

	T. S. Eliot	*The Age*
1911	Studies Sanskrit and Oriental philosophy at Harvard.	Hoffmannsthal's *Everyman*. Stravinsky's *Petrouchka* produced.
1912		Claudel's *The Tidings Brought to Mary*. Thomas Mann's *Death in Venice*.
1913		Stravinsky's *The Rite of Spring* produced.
1914	Studies in Germany, then England. June 26: Marriage.	World War I begins.
1916		Easter Rising leaders executed in Dublin. Death of Henry James.
1917	*Prufrock and Other Observations. Ezra Pound: his Metric and Poetry.*	Russian revolution. Yeats's *At the Hawk's Well.*
1918		American pacifist and socialist Eugene Debs imprisoned. November 11: Armistice signed. World War I ends. Spengler's *Decline of the West* (Volume I).
1920	*Poems; The Sacred Wood.*	First assembly of the League of Nations. Weston's *From Ritual to Romance.*
1922	*The Waste Land;* first issue of *The Criterion.*	Joyce's *Ulysses,* Rilke's *Duino Elegies,* Cummings' *The Enormous Room,* Hoffmannsthal's *The Great Theatre of the World.* Death of Marcel Proust.
1924	*Homage to John Dryden.*	Lenin succeeded by Stalin. Shaw's *St. Joan* performed. Thomas Mann's *The Magic Mountain.*
1925	*Poems 1909–1925.*	Alban Berg's *Wozzek* performed.
1926	Eliot introduces his mother's dramatic poem *Savonarola.*	British General Strike.

T. S. Eliot	The Age
1927 Eliot is confirmed into the Church of England and assumes British citizenship.	Sacco and Vanzetti, radicals, executed in Boston.
1928 *For Lancelot Andrewes.*	Brecht's *The Threepenny Opera* produced. O'Casey's *The Silver Tassie* published.
1929 *Dante.*	Beginning of the Depression. Mann wins Nobel prize.
1930 *Ash Wednesday.*	Vladimir Mayakovsky, charged as a Trotskyite, commits suicide. Gandhi leads salt march defying government salt monopoly and is imprisoned with many followers. André Obey's *Noah* completed.
1931 *Thoughts after Lambeth.*	Sino-Japanese conflict in Manchuria. O'Neill's *Mourning Becomes Electra.* Cummings' "i sing of olaf" (poem on the torture and death of a conscientious objector).
1932 *Sweeney Agonistes.* Eliot is Charles Eliot Norton Professor of Poetry at Harvard.	Gandhi, reimprisoned, wins rights for Untouchables by "fast unto death." Rouault's *Christ Mocked by Soldiers* completed. Auden's *The Orators.*
1933 *The Use of Poetry and the Use of Criticism.*	Hitler leads National Socialists to power. Mann leaves Germany.
1934 *Sweeney Agonistes* produced by the Group Theatre, London. May 28: *The Rock* opens at Sadlers Wells Theatre, London, and is published May 31. *After Strange Gods* (The Page-Barbour Lectures at the University of Virginia, 1933).	Blood purge in Germany. Einstein deprived of German citizenship and property. German Confessional Church formed to resist Hitler's interference in ecclesiastical affairs. Nazi dictatorship of Adolf Hitler. Kirov, Leningrad party secretary, murdered in U.S.S.R. Stalin starts the great purges. Cocteau's *The Infernal Machine* produced.

T. S. Eliot	*The Age*
1935	May 10: *Murder in the Cathedral* published at Canterbury for sale at performances. June 13: First (complete) edition published in London by Faber and Faber. September 19: First American edition published in New York by Harcourt, Brace and Company. June 15: Performed in the Chapter House of Canterbury Cathedral. November 1: Performed at Mercury Theatre, London.	Italy attacks Ethiopia and Abyssinia. Hitler repudiates military clauses of Treaty of Versailles, reintroducing conscription and re-arming Germany. Giradoux's *The Trojan War Will Not Take Place* produced. Soviet writers and artists (J. Eisenstein, Isaac Babel, B. Pilnyak and others) perish in Russian concentration camps (1935–1938). Auden's *The Dog Beneath the Skin.*
1936	January: Second English edition, conforming with Mercury Theatre production. Second American edition. March 20: Performed by Federal Theatre Project at Manhattan Theater, New York. October 30: Performed at the Duchess Theatre in London's West End. *Collected Poems, 1909–1935,* including "Burnt Norton."	German armies enter Rhineland. Berlin-Rome Axis formed. Japan joins Axis. Franco receives support from Axis. Spanish Civil War. Garcia Lorca's *The House of Bernarda Alba* completed. Lorca executed by Spanish terrorists. Mann deprived of German citizenship.
1937	June 8: *Murder in the Cathedral* opens at the Old Vic, London. August: Third English edition, in which Fourth Knight's speeches are reassigned. Hungarian version, *"Gyilkosság A Katedrálisban"* performed.	July: Arrest of Pastor Martin Niemoeller of the German Confessional Church. Picasso's "Guernica" presents the tragedy of the Spanish Civil War. Soviet-Finnish War. Auden's *The Ascent of F6* produced.
1938	September: Fourth English edition, with further rearrangements and deletions.	Germany annexes Austria. Freud leaves Vienna when Nazis take the city. Conference of Munich. Brecht's *Fear and Trembling of the Third Reich* produced. Camus' *Caligula* completed. Paul Hindemith leaves Germany when his music is attacked. Soviet-German non-aggression pact.

T. S. Eliot	The Age
1939	March 21: *The Family Reunion* performed at the Westminister Theatre, London, and published that day. *The Idea of a Christian Society*.	World War II begins. Six million European Jews annihilated by Nazi Germany (1939–45). Freud dies in London.
1940		August 8: Germans open the battle of Britain.
1943	*Four Quartets* (1936, 1940, 1941, 1942).	Sixty thousand perish in uprising in Warsaw Ghetto.
1944	*Meurtre dans la Cathédrale*, translated by Henri Fluchère.	June 6: D-day. Landing in Normandy begins Allied reconquest of Western Europe. Plot against Hitler fails; plotters executed. Dietrich Bonhoeffer executed. Anouilh's *Antigone*, Sartre's *No Exit* produced.
1945	Produced by Jean Vilar at the Vieux-Colombier, Paris, 1945–46.	April 29: American troops liberate Dachau concentration camp. United States devastates Hiroshima (August 6) and Nagasaki (August 9) with atomic bombs. End of War. Nuremberg trials (1945–46) begin. United Nations charter enters into force (October 24).
1947	Death of first wife after a long illness. *Mord in Dom*, translation by R. A. Schroeder, opens at Cologne, Goettingen, and Munich.	Partition of India. Indian independence.
1948	Eliot receives Nobel prize and Order of Merit. *Notes Toward the Definition of Culture*.	January 10: Gandhi assassinated by Hindu patriot for tolerance toward Moslems. Sartre's *Dirty Hands* completed.
1949	August 22: *The Cocktail Party* performed at the Lyceum Theatre, Edinburgh.	Cardinal Joseph Mindszenty sentenced to life imprisonment for "espionage" in Communist Hungary.
1950	*The Cocktail Party*.	Senator Joseph McCarthy hunts for "Communists" in government and other institutions, in-

T. S. Eliot

The Age

cluding the churches. The McCarran-Nixon bill hits at rights of "subversives." Korean War (1950–53).

1951 Premiere at Venice of film *Murder in the Cathedral* produced by George Hoellering. *Poetry and Drama.*

April 11: General Douglas MacArthur, commander of United Nations forces, removed by President Truman.

1952 *The Film of Murder in the Cathedral* by T. S. Eliot and George Hoellering published in New York by Harcourt, Brace and Company.

November 1: United States explodes the first hydrogen bomb. Beckett's *Waiting for Godot.*

1953 August 25: *The Confidential Clerk* performed at the Lyceum Theatre, Edinburgh.

Death of Joseph Stalin.

1954 *Religious Drama, Medieval and Modern. The Confidential Clerk.*

May 17: U.S. Supreme Court declares segregation in public schools unconstitutional. July 20: The Convention of Geneva ends Indo-Chinese War, divides Vietnam, and provides for reunification by elections within two years.

1955 Eliot lectures on "Goethe as the Sage" at Hamburg University on receiving the Hanseatic Goethe Prize for 1954. *The Literature of Politics,* lecture at Conservative Political Centre.

December 1: Mrs. Rosa Parks refuses to give up her seat in the Cleveland Avenue bus, Montgomery, Alabama. December 5: The Montgomery bus boycott begins.

1956 *The Frontiers of Criticism,* the Gideon Seymour lecture at the University of Minnesota.

February: Khrushchev's "secret speech" against Stalin at the twentieth Party congress. Cardinal Mindszenty liberated. Conflict between Egypt and Israel, France and Great Britain over control of Suez Canal. November 4: Russian military intervention suppresses Hungarian revolt.

1957 January 10: Eliot is married to Valerie Fletcher. *On Poetry and Poets.*

	T. S. Eliot	*The Age*
1958	August 25: *The Elder States-man* performed at the Lyceum Theatre, Edinburgh. Operatic version of *Murder in the Cathedral*, score by Ildebrando Pizzetti, staged.	Imre Nagy, former prime minister of Hungary, executed. Anouilh's *Becket* completed. Ezra Pound leaves St. Elizabeth's Hospital after 1945 indictment for treason is dismissed.
1959		First Sputnik.
1960		Fry's *Curtmantle*.
1963		June 12: Medgar Evers, N.A.A.C.P. official, assassinated in Jackson, Mississippi. William L. Moore, white civil rights worker, assassinated in Atlanta, Alabama. August 28: 200,000 in civil rights March on Washington. September 15: Negro Baptist church in Birmingham, Alabama, bombed, killing four girls. President Ngo Dinh Diem and his brother Ngo Dinh Nhu repress Buddhist anti-war demonstrators. Meet death November 1 after military coup takes over government. November 22: President John F. Kennedy assassinated in Dallas, Texas.
1964	*Knowledge and Experience in the Philosophy of F. H. Bradley.*	June 21: James Chaney, Andrew Goodman, and Michael Schwerner, civil rights workers, lynched in Philadelphia, Mississippi. Bodies found in earthen dam 44 days later. October 14: Nikita Khrushchev replaced as first secretary and premier.
1965	January 4: T. S. Eliot dies in London. *To Criticize the Critic.*	February 21: Malcolm X, black nationalist, shot to death by members of rival faction while addressing Harlem rally.
1967	*Poems Written in Early Youth.*	May 16: Miss Pham Thi Mai, appealing for peace in Viet-

T. S. Eliot   *The Age*

		nam, immolates herself in Saigon.
1968		March: American infantry unit massacres unarmed Vietnamese civilians in sweep through hamlet (Mylai 4) near Songmy. April 4: The Rev. Martin Luther King, Jr., assassinated in Memphis, Tennessee. June 6: Senator Robert F. Kennedy assassinated in Los Angeles, California. Russia invades Czechoslovakia.
1969		January: Jiri Palach, Czech student protesting against Soviet invasion, immolates himself in Prague. December 4: Fred Hampton, Chairman of Illinois Black Panthers, shot to death by police in Chicago. First man on the moon.
1970	September 25: For the first time, *Murder in the Cathedral* is performed in the nave of Canterbury Cathedral, in a production by E. Martin Browne, as part of the Canterbury Festival, marking the 800th anniversary of the death of Becket.	Biafran war ends after death of up to 2,000,000, largely by starvation. Cambodian troops kill 1000 Vietnamese in mass executions. April 30: President Nixon sends American combat troops into Cambodia. Protests erupt on campuses throughout nation. May 4: Allison Krause, Jeffrey Glenn Miller, Sandra Lee Scheuer, and William K. Schroeder are killed when National Guardsmen open fire on students at Kent State University, Ohio. May 11: Six blacks are killed in suppression of riots in Augusta, Georgia. May 15: Philip L. Gibbs and James Earl Green are killed when police open fire on students at Jackson State College, Mississippi.

Notes on the Editor and Contributors

DAVID R. CLARK is Professor of English at the University of Massachusetts, author of *W. B. Yeats and the Theatre of Desolate Reality*, and co-editor of *Druid Craft: The Writing of 'The Shadowy Waters,'* first volume in the series *Manuscripts of W. B. Yeats* of which he is general editor.

J. T. BOULTON is Professor of Literature at the University of Nottingham. His publications include an edition of Edmund Burke's *Philosophical Enquiry into . . . the Sublime and Beautiful; The Language of Politics in the Age of Wilkes and Burke; Daniel Defoe: Selected Verse and Prose; Lawrence in Love;* and an early version of Lawrence's "Odour of Chrysanthemums" in *Renaissance and Modern Studies*. He has finished a volume on Samuel Johnson for the Routledge "Critical Heritage" series.

E. MARTIN BROWNE directed the first productions of all of Eliot's plays in Britain and most of them in New York. He also acted as consultant in their creation and has recorded the process in *The Making of T. S. Eliot's Plays*. He has been leader of the revival of religious drama in Britain, producing both new work and the pioneer revival of a Mystery Cycle at York from 1951. His series of "New Plays by Poets" at the Mercury Theatre, London, 1945-48, introduced Christopher Fry, Ronald Duncan, and other writers to the stage. He was Director of the British Drama League, 1948-57 and is President of RADIUS (the Religious Drama Society of Great Britain). From 1956-62 he was Visiting Professor in Religious Drama at Union Theological Seminary. In the autumn of 1970 he directed the production of *Murder in the Cathedral* at the special Canterbury Festival memorializing the 800th anniversary of Becket's death.

FRANCIS FERGUSSON is University Professor of Comparative Literature at Rutgers University and author of *The Idea of a Theater, Dante's Drama of the Mind,* and *The Human Image in Dramatic Literature*.

DAVID E. JONES is Associate Professor of Theatre, University of Utah. He is author of *The Plays of T. S. Eliot* and of essays on the drama.

H. Z. MACCOBY is Head of the English Department of the Feltham School, Feltham, Middlesex, and author of "Two Notes on 'Ash Wednesday' "; "Two

Notes on 'Murder in the Cathedral' "; "A Commentary on 'Burnt Norton,' I"; "A Commentary on 'Burnt Norton,' II"; "Difficulties in the Plot of 'Family Reunion' "; " 'The Family Reunion' and Kipling's 'The House Surgeon' "— all in *Notes and Queries;* "An Interpretation of 'Mr. Eliot's Sunday Morning Service' " in *The Critical Survey;* and other articles in *Midstream, New Testament Studies,* and *The Jewish Quarterly.*

Louis L. Martz is Douglas Tracy Smith Professor of English and American Literature at Yale University and author of *The Poetry of Meditation, The Paradise Within, The Poem of the Mind,* and *The Wit of Love.*

Robert N. Shorter is Associate Professor of English at Wake Forest University and the author of "Becket as Job." A medievalist, he is presently working on a book-length study of Chaucer's *Troilus and Criseyde.*

Kristian Smidt, Professor of English at the University of Oslo, is the author of *James Joyce and the Cultic Use of Fiction, Poetry and Belief in the Works of T. S. Eliot, Iniurious Imposters and Richard III,* and *T. S. Eliot and W. B. Yeats.*

Carol H. Smith is Associate Professor of English at Douglass College, Rutgers University. She is author of *T. S. Eliot's Dramatic Theory and Practice* and of essays on Eliot.

Grover C. Smith is Professor of English at Duke University. He is author of *T. S. Eliot's Poetry and Plays* and editor of *Josiah Royce's Seminar, 1913–1914.*

William V. Spanos is Assistant Professor of English at the State University of New York at Binghamton, editor of *A Casebook on Existentialism,* author of *The Christian Tradition in Modern Verse Drama,* and of essays on Yeats, Pound, and others. He is presently writing about Charles Williams and about Imagism.

Selected Bibliography

Braybrook, Neville. *T. S. Eliot: A Symposium for His Seventieth Birthday*. London: Rupert Hart-Davis, 1958. Includes essays by E. Martin Browne, who produced *Murder in the Cathedral*, pp. 57–69, Robert Speaight, who acted the part of Becket, pp. 70–78, George Hoellering, who produced the film version, pp. 81–84, and others.

Donoghue, Denis. *The Third Voice: Modern British and American Verse Drama*. Princeton, New Jersey: Princeton University Press, 1959, pp. 76–93. A keen criticism, finding structural flaws and an evasion of the problems of dramatic verse.

Gardner, Helen. *The Art of T. S. Eliot*. New York: E. P. Dutton & Co., 1959, pp. 127–139. First published in 1950. Finds the drama in the Chorus, rather than in Thomas, who has no inner development.

Kenner, Hugh. *The Invisible Poet: T. S. Eliot*. New York: McDowell, Obolensky, 1959, pp. 276–285. Brief, brilliant analysis of Eliot's attempt to face his dramatic problems.

Kornbluth, Martin L., "A Twentieth-century *Everyman*," *College English*, XXI (1959), 26–29. Develops the resemblances between *Murder in the Cathedral* and *Everyman*.

Martz, Louis L., "The Saint as Tragic Hero: *Saint Joan* and *Murder in the Cathedral*," in Cleanth Brooks, ed., *Tragic Themes in Western Literature*. New Haven: Yale University Press, 1955, pp. 150–78. Valuable comments on the structure. Finds the play a "strongly affirmative tragedy."

Mason, W. H. *Murder in the Cathedral (T. S. Eliot)*. Oxford: Basil Blackwell and Mott, 1962. New York: Barnes & Noble, 1963. Unpretentious, clear, thorough, extremely helpful notes on all elements of the play.

Maxwell, D. E. S. *The Poetry of T. S. Eliot*. London: Routledge & Kegan Paul, 1952. Third impression, 1958, pp. 181–89. Argues that Thomas is not a passive character, but that the form of the play, influenced by the morality plays and Greek tragedy, deemphasizes character.

Peter, John, *"Murder in the Cathedral," The Sewanee Review,* LXI, 3 (Summer 1953), 362–383. Reprinted in *T. S. Eliot: A Collection of Critical Essays,* ed. Hugh Kenner. Englewood Cliffs, N. J.: Prentice-Hall, Inc., 1962, pp. 155–72. Excellent analysis. Ranks *Murder in the Cathedral* above *The Family Reunion* and *The Cocktail Party* and far above Tennyson's *Becket.*

Ransom, John Crowe. *The World's Body.* Baton Rouge: Louisiana State University Press, 1968. First published 1938. An early review, "A Cathedralist Looks at Murder," pp. 166–72, finds the writing unsure and inconsistent in contrast to that of *Samson Agonistes.* A 1968 "Postscript," pp. 351–90, apologizes without retracting. Ransom is brilliant, charming, lovable, as always.

Spencer, Theodore, "On 'Murder in the Cathedral,' " *The Harvard Advocate,* CXXV, 3 (December 1938), pp. 21–22. Brief, central essay, finds that the characters represent four different levels of reality.

Williams, Raymond. *Drama from Ibsen to Eliot.* London: Chatto & Windus, 1952, pp. 227–31. Dramatic pattern, by being fully articulated in the verse, controls visual effects and character. *Murder in the Cathedral* is a triumphant "discovery of an adequate form for serious drama."

TWENTIETH CENTURY
INTERPRETATIONS

Maynard Mack, *Series Editor*
Yale University

NOW AVAILABLE
Collections of Critical Essays
ON

Adventures of Huckleberry Finn
All for Love
The Ambassadors
Arrowsmith
As You Like It
Bleak House
The Book of Job
Boswell's Life of Johnson
The Castle
Coriolanus
Doctor Faustus
Don Juan
Dubliners
The Duchess of Malfi
Endgame
Euripides' Alcestis
The Eve of St. Agnes
The Fall of the House of Usher
A Farewell to Arms
The Frogs

(*continued on next page*)

(continued from previous page)

GRAY'S ELEGY
THE GREAT GATSBY
GULLIVER'S TRAVELS
HAMLET
HARD TIMES
HENRY IV, PART TWO
HENRY V
THE ICEMAN COMETH
JULIUS CAESAR
KEATS'S ODES
LIGHT IN AUGUST
LORD JIM
MAJOR BARBARA
MEASURE FOR MEASURE
THE MERCHANT OF VENICE
MOLL FLANDERS
MOLLOY, MALONE DIES, THE UNNAMABLE
MUCH ADO ABOUT NOTHING
MURDER IN THE CATHEDRAL
THE NIGGER OF THE "NARCISSUS"
OEDIPUS REX
THE OLD MAN AND THE SEA
PAMELA
A PASSAGE TO INDIA
THE PLAYBOY OF THE WESTERN WORLD
POE'S TALES
THE PORTRAIT OF A LADY
A PORTRAIT OF THE ARTIST AS A YOUNG MAN
THE PRAISE OF FOLLY
PRIDE AND PREJUDICE
THE RAINBOW
THE RAPE OF THE LOCK
THE RIME OF THE ANCIENT MARINER
ROBINSON CRUSOE
ROMEO AND JULIET
SAMSON AGONISTES
THE SCARLET LETTER
SIR GAWAIN AND THE GREEN KNIGHT
SONGS OF INNOCENCE AND OF EXPERIENCE

(continued from previous page)

THE SOUND AND THE FURY
THE TEMPEST
TESS OF THE D'URBERVILLES
TOM JONES
TO THE LIGHTHOUSE
THE TURN OF THE SCREW
TWELFTH KNIGHT
UTOPIA
VANITY FAIR
WALDEN
THE WASTE LAND
WOMEN IN LOVE
WUTHERING HEIGHTS